The Best
Low-Fat, No-Sugar
Bread Machine
Cookbook Ever

The Best Low-Fat, No-Sugar Bread Machine Cookbook Ever

Madge Rosenberg

A John Boswell Associates/King Hill Productions Book
HarperCollins *Publishers*

Design: Barbara Cohen Aronica
Index: Maro Riofrancos

Library of Congress Cataloging-in-Publication Data

Rosenberg, Madge.
   The best, low-fat, no-sugar bread machine cookbook ever / Madge Rosenberg.—1st ed.
      p.   cm.
   "A John Boswell Associates/King Hill Productions book."
   Includes index.
   ISBN 0-06-017174-X
   1. Bread.   2. Automatic bread machines.   3. Low-fat diet—Recipes.
4. Sugar-free diet—Recipes.   I. Title.
TX769.R794   1995
641.8'15—dc20   95-7034

---

96 97 98 99 HC 10 9 8 7 6 5

Dedication

To Natalie Andersen, my sister, for her encouragement, organization, commitment, and love of good food. She tested and tasted everything and is still a size 8.

Thanks to Barry for the most precious gifts: time and love. To Peter for letting me stand on his shoulders and peek out of the technology trough. And to Lili and Jojo, the independent young women who set an example for their mother.

Contents

Set the dial the night before and wake up to such unbelievably low-fat, no-sugar-added treats as Bran Muffin Bread, Cinnamon-Raisin Bread, and Morning Mocha Bread. Or enjoy a cup of coffee with Cranberry Buns or Onion Wheatberry Bagels.

Sturdy for slicing and perfect pairings with tasty lean fillings, these loaves include Buttermilk Corn Bread, Low-Fat Challah, Sourdough Rye Bread, Roasted Onion and Orange Whole Wheat Bread, and Mushroom and Barley Bread.

Introduction

The Bread Machine as a Lean Machine

If you want to ingest less cholesterol and fewer calories and enrich your diet with more vitamins, protein, and minerals, my suggestion is to eat good bread. Of course, being a professional baker, I am slightly prejudiced, but it is a fact that fresh bread, loaded with fiber and fruits, perfumed with spices, very low in fat, and containing no refined sugar, makes a major contribution to a healthy diet. Bread is greater than the sum of its basic parts: flour, water, yeast, and salt. What other food gives so much satisfaction from such humble ingredients so miraculously transformed? And making bread in a bread machine is almost as magical as making fire by striking a match.

In a bread machine you can make bread tailored to your diet, tastes, means, and schedule. Put in what you want and like; omit ingredients, such as fat and sugar, that you wish to avoid. Since you eat the bread at its freshest, no preservatives are necessary, no synthetic dough conditioners or emulsifiers, not even the sugar and fats that commercial bakers often must add to make breads stay soft and last longer. You can eat bread lean and almost sugar-free because you eat it fresh, at its height in food value.

If you need calcium, add it to your bread with nonfat dry milk and nonfat yogurt without adding fat. If you need fiber, add flavorful fruits and vegetables. Even moist, flavor-rich, salt-free bread is possible and, with a machine, easy to fit into a busy daily routine. I include a chapter on good tasting, salt-free breads, which are often hard to find for people on low-sodium diets.

Although many of the breads taste rich enough for dessert, I never used an egg yolk or even unwrapped a stick of butter or margarine. Instead, these recipes are luxurious in nutritious grains, in the natural sweetness of fresh and dried fruits, in the savor of seasonal vegetables and sensuous spices.

Bread has become so stylish that many multistarred restaurants acknowledge their bread suppliers on their menus and often a selection of breads in the manner in which they used to present French pastries. The best American artisanal bread bakers have formed the Bread Bakers Guild around their passion for wonderful bread. And the latest in expensive, custom-kitchen designs includes built-in, pale wood bread boxes. Bread is definitely back, and in the United States it is better than ever. But the best bread is still the fresh bread you bake yourself, and the best baker is you with the help of your bread machine.

About the Ingredients

Dry Yeast Yeast is made of tiny plants that change food—especially gluten and sugars—into carbon dioxide, causing the bread to rise. Now there is a choice of dry yeasts on the market: active dry yeast, bread machine yeast, instant yeast, and rapid-rise yeast. The finer the granules, the quicker the yeast dissolves, and the more "instant" its action. Not every type is available everywhere. We did not find much difference between the breads produced with ordinary active dry yeast, which is readily available everywhere, and bread machine yeast, which is available only in some parts of the country. Keep all yeast in the refrigerator. Do not use cake (fresh) yeast in bread machines.

Yeast will die in water that is hotter than 115 degrees. Cold water will slow the action of the yeast. Liquids added to yeast should be close to body temperature (98.6 degrees); dry ingredients should be at room temperature. Since salt slows the yeast and can kill it, add the salt with the liquids to protect the yeast.

Barley Malt Syrup This syrup is made by sprouting and drying barley grain and caramelizing its sugar. It adds a rich, barely sweet taste, while encouraging the yeast and sourdough to rise and produce richer, moister bread. It is available in some health food stores or by mail order from the sources on page 12.

Caramel Coloring Most really dark breads are colored with burned sugar or caramel syrup. It sweetens bread only slightly, but adds moisture as well as color. Making your own will ruin a pot and possibly your kitchen. Mail-order sources are listed on page 12.

In Place of Fats Oils, butter, lard, egg yolks, and nuts all make bread softer and preserve it longer. Since a gram of fat has 9 calories and a gram of protein has 4 calories, you can see why fat is fattening. And fat is suspected of contributing to heart disease and some cancers. I do not use fats in this book. Instead, potatoes, prunes, bananas, and figs soften the dough while providing fiber, vitamins, and minerals as well as lots of flavor. Use nonstick pots and pans whenever possible. When a pan needs to be oiled, use vegetable oil cooking spray.

Salt Salt not only adds flavor, it governs the power of the yeast. Too much salt kills the yeast; too little lets dough rise too much and then fall before it finishes baking. Salt is also a preservative. In order to cut back on salt, I have reduced the amount of yeast used in the recipes in this book. Salt-free breads are possible—you will find a whole chapter—because the breads are so fresh that they can get away without salt as a preservative.

Sourdough Starter Your sourdough starter becomes like a pet—you watch over it and feed it. It takes at least a week to develop flour and water into a starter. But once made, and continually fed, it will keep for years. Mail-order sources for sourdough starter are on page 12.

To make sourdough starter: In a large glass or plastic container, mix 1 cup of flour with 1 cup of water and a pinch of dry yeast. Stir until creamy, loosely cover, and leave at room temperature (not above 80 degrees) for a week.

After the first week, refrigerate the sourdough starter. The solids will separate from the liquid, so stir before using and bring the starter up to the right temperature for the bread machine by making the water in the recipe just warmer than body temperature and mixing the two together before using. At least once a week, use your starter or discard ½ cup of it and replenish with equal amounts of flour and water stirred together until they are smooth and creamy. This keeps the starter fresh and active.

Sourdough starter is a living culture that bubbles and smells strange. Different strains of yeast in the air work on the sour. Sours made from the same ingredients vary from place to place because of the ambient conditions. No one has made San Francisco sourdough in the Midwest yet, although commercial bakers have tried.

Sweeteners Forget sugars—this book uses fresh and dried fruit, sugar-free preserves, and fruit juice concentrates to balance the flavors and help the bread to brown.

Wheat Bread flour is made from high-gluten or hard wheat without its germ or bran, but containing all the gluten from the grain. It rises better than any other flour and gives the bread a sturdy structure, especially when vegetables and fruits are added.

Whole wheat flour has the bran and the germ, but a lower proportion of gluten. It rises, but not as well as bread flour. In some recipes, extracted vital wheat gluten is added to help the bread rise.

Wheat bran is the outside of the wheat kernel. It contains the vitamins and fiber, but not the gluten. It is sold in health food stores and in the flour or grain section of large supermarkets.

Wheat germ is the center of the wheat kernel, which contains the oils and many nutrients. It is sold in jars and should be refrigerated once the jar is opened, to keep it from becoming rancid because of its high oil content.

Wheatberries are the kernels of wheat. They have the crunch and taste of nuts and add to the flavor and nutritional value of bread.

To cook wheatberries: Bring ½ cup water to a boil in a small saucepan. Add ¼ cup wheatberries. Reduce the heat to low, cover, and simmer 30 minutes. If all of the water has not been absorbed, drain the wheatberries. Yield: ½ cup cooked wheatberries.

Vital wheat gluten is wheat flour with the starch removed. It helps bread rise. It is sold in health food stores.

Other Flours and Grains

Amaranth is a nutty, high-protein grain from Central America. Since it is very low in gluten, use small quantities along with a large amount of wheat flour.

Barley, thought to be the oldest cultivated grain, has little gluten but contributes niacin and potassium as well as texture and fiber to the dough. Barley flakes are made by steaming and flattening the grain. Hulled or hulless barley is interchangeable in breads. Pearled barley has had its hull and some of its nutrients removed.

Buckwheat groats, also known as *kasha,* is actually an herb, not a grain. Both ground and whole, buckwheat adds a nutty taste and fiber to breads.

To cook buckwheat groats: Bring ½ cup water to a boil in a small saucepan. Add ¼ cup groats. Reduce the heat to low, cover, and simmer 10 minutes. Yield: ½ cup cooked groats.

Cornmeal adds its own slightly sweet flavor, crumbly texture, and sunny color to bread if you use yellow cornmeal, as I do. Stone-ground meal is more distinctive, but the supermarket variety will serve just as well in these recipes.

Oatmeal is just regular, old-fashioned oatmeal, or rolled oats, the same oats that you use for breakfast cereal. (Do not use instant oatmeal.) Oatmeal adds flavor and fiber and contains its own oat bran. Toast oatmeal lightly in a 350 degree oven 5 minutes to intensify the flavor.

Quinoa is a high-protein, pearly grain from Peru, recently popularized in the United States for its nutritional value.

Rye flour has a fair amount of protein and flavor, but little gluten to give bread structure. Less than a third of the flour content of bread should be rye; the rest should be wheat flour.

Helpful Hints

1. Always buy pitted dried fruit, which means the pits have been removed. Double check to make sure that there are no pits left. If a pit gets into the bread machine, it may scratch the surface of the bread pan and blade.

2. Before using nuts and seeds, toast them lightly in a 350 degree oven or in a hot, dry frying pan 3 to 5 minutes to bring out the flavor and make your house smell wonderful. Let cool before using.

3. Before you slice or juice an orange or a lemon, peel off the zest, the colored part of the skin, with a swivel-bladed vegetable peeler. Save it for the many recipes that call for oranges or lemon zest.

4. If you are using just the zest of a lemon in a bread, rub the flesh of the lemon on your hands to eliminate the odor of garlic or onion, and rub it under your fingernails to whiten them.

5. When you remove baked bread from the machine, keep the loaf inverted until it is just cool enough to handle; then check to be sure the kneading blade has not remained in the loaf. If it has, remove it before turning the bread right side up. If you slice the bread with the blade still in it, you will scrape the blade and remove some of the nonstick coating.

6. To store bread, place it in a plastic bag with a rib of celery to keep it fresher. The new resealable plastic bags with tiny holes are best. Store in a cool, dry place. I find that bread gets soggy in the refrigerator.

Freezing

To freeze baked bread, let the loaf cool completely. Wrap the whole unsliced bread in plastic wrap or foil, forcing out as much air as possible. Defrost the bread in its wrapping for 2 hours or overnight. Unwrap and let stand for another hour so that it will not be soggy. For quicker thawing, slice the bread before freezing.

To warm defrosted bread, place it in a preheated 300 degree oven 15 minutes, or less if it is sliced. Or microwave according to the oven manufacturer's directions. If you want to freeze unbaked dough that has completed the dough cycle in the bread machine, brush it lightly with oil, wrap in plastic, and freeze for no more than 2 days. The yeast gradually loses its ability to rise. To defrost, loosen the wrapping and defrost for a few hours or overnight in the refrigerator. When completely defrosted, leave at room temperature in a draft-free place to rise. Do not leave the dough unrefrigerated while defrosting, or the outside will rise too much before the inside defrosts.

Adding Ingredients to Your Bread Machine

Know your machine before you begin. Read your owner's manual, because bread machines differ. Some begin by adding the liquid ingredients, then the dry, and lastly the yeast. Others begin with the yeast and other dry ingredients and add the liquids last. Yeast is always kept separate from liquids until the processing begins. While a few machines require that all ingredients be at room temperature before they go into the machine, other machines warm everything to an ideal temperature in the machine.

Too much liquid produces soggy bread, often with a sunken crater in the center. Too much flour makes a heavy, dry bread. Flours vary in the amount of water they absorb. If the flour is low in gluten and absorbs less water, use an extra tablespoon or two of flour to make a firm dough, or find a bread flour high in gluten that will work best in these recipes.

Machines with longer kneading and rising times turn out stronger, less delicate breads and can handle more whole grain flours. They are a little more tolerant.

Measuring

Dry Ingredients Measure over a plate or paper towel. Spoon flours and grains and spices into dry measuring cups or spoons until overflowing. Do not press down. Level by sweeping the excess off with a spatula or straight-edge knife.

Flavorings and Fillers These include fruits, vegetables, yogurt cheese, and whole grains. Press firmly into a dry measuring cup or spoon. Level off the excess with a spatula or straight-edge knife.

Liquids Use standard liquid measuring cups and spoons. Check measurements at eye level.

About the Bread Machines

More than 3 million bread machines have been sold in the United States in the past 3 years. Yeast and flour producers are making special strains and grinds just for bread machines. Not only has the demand for machines grown steadily, but according to Fleischmann's Yeast research, "more than half of the owners bake as much or more frequently two to three years after buying their machines."

I found that all of the machines did a good job on the basic bread cycle, except when there was little bread flour and a great deal of whole wheat and low-gluten grains. The whole wheat cycle, which gives more kneading and rising time, worked best on these difficult breads. I did not like sweet bread cycles, even when fruits were included in the dough. Since my doughs are so lean, the sweet bread cycle does not brown the loaves enough for my taste. Machines that do not have solid bottoms, such as the DAK and Welbilt, do not work well for doughs that are finished outside of the machine.

All of the following machines have delayed timers, nonstick interior finishes, and white plastic exteriors. With the above considerations taken into account, they all make good bread.

BLACK AND DECKER
This very quiet, 1½-pound machine mixes additional ingredients in well, even though it does not have a timer to tell you when to add them. It has a basic 4-hour cycle and a 3-hour "fresh milk cycle."

DAK
This machine is available only through the DAK Industries catalog out of California. The 1-pound model is one of the least expensive available, and DAK some-

times sells reconditioned models. The Turbo Baker II has a domed glass top and makes and bakes a 1½-pound loaf in 2½ hours.

HITACHI

The Hitachi is the only machine we tried that lets you make a ½-pound, 1-pound, 1½-pound, or 2-pound loaf in the same machine. It will also make jam and steam rice. The basic cycle produces crusty loaves.

PANASONIC OR NATIONAL

In 3 hours (rapid) or 4 hours (regular), this machine bakes a very crusty bread. The whole wheat cycle is especially good for breads with a lot of low-gluten flours and little bread flour. The basic dough cycle takes over 2 hours. There is no buzzer to tell you when to add extra ingredients. It is one of the sturdiest of all the machines we used, and this is the only model that makes a traditional horizontal loaf.

REGAL

The "raisin bread cycle" on the Regal, which has a buzzer to signal the addition of fruit and nuts, and the "bread cycle" take 3 hours and 40 minutes, including a 20-minute cool down. The "rapid" cycle takes just under 3 hours for a 1-pound loaf with a light crust.

SANYO

The Bread Factory Plus makes a 1-pound loaf on French, sweet, basic, and either rapid or regular whole wheat cycles in 3 to 4 hours. It distributes added raisins and nuts evenly without pulverizing them. This machine stops when the lid is raised, a nice safety feature, and it has a small viewing window in the top.

TRILLIUM BREADMAN

In a 2½-hour cycle, the Breadman produces bread with an excellent crust. It has a buzzer to signal additions and is well priced. There is a viewing window in the top, a 3-year warranty, and an instructional video.

WELBILT

The Welbilt is my original bread machine, more than 300 breads old. This is one of the originals, with a basic bread and dough cycle, and even the dough cycle has a beeper for adding ingredients. It makes a tall round loaf. The 1½-pound Welbilt has a domed glass top and a 4-hour bread cycle. The 1-pound loaf takes less than 2½ hours.

WESTBEND

So far, this is the only machine made in the U.S.A. It has a 3-hour "warmer" cycle that keeps the bread moist once it is baked. The same machine will make a 1- or 1½-pound loaf on 3- to 3-hour-and-40-minute cycles. It comes with an instructional video.

ZOJIRUSHI

This is a substantial, sturdy machine that has a tall, slim bread pan and an attractive exterior. It is the only machine that has a "Homemade Menu" that you can program yourself. It has a glass top for viewing the progress of the bread and a crumb tray for easy cleaning. There are raisin, French, quick bread, dough, cake, and jam cycles. It makes a crusty loaf.

As I write, more machines are on the way from Betty Crocker and Toastmaster.

Mail-Order Sources for Ingredients

FLOURS AND GRAINS

Arrowhead Mills
110 South Lawton
Hereford, TX 79045
(800) 749-0730

Deer Valley Farm
Box 173
Guilford, NY 13780-0173
(607) 764-8556

King Arthur Flour
Route 5 South
Norwich, VT 05055
(800) 827-6836

Shiloh Farms
P.O. Box 97
Sulphur Springs, AR 72768-0097
(800) 362-6832

Tadco/Niblack
900 Jefferson Road, Bldg. 5
Rochester, NY 14623
(800) 724-8883

Walnut Acres
Penns Creek, PA 17862
(800) 433-3998

SOURDOUGH STARTER
King Arthur Flour

**BARLEY MALT SYRUP
AND CARAMEL COLORING**
King Arthur Flour
Tadco/Niblack

Chapter One

Breakfast Breads

Warm bread from your bread machine is the best thing to happen to breakfast since the invention of the bagel. The smell of freshly baked bread is the nicest way to lure you from your bed on the grayest morning. Whether you eat a thick chunk out of your hand on the run or sit down to a toasted slice with your favorite spread or low-fat cheese, a fresh bagel, bun, or loaf of warm bread makes breakfast better.

For starting the day right, the breads in this chapter are largely high in protein, minerals, and fiber-rich grains but low in fat and free of sugar. They toast well for serving with an egg-white omelet or all-fruit jam. The buns are soft and just sweet enough to replace muffins in the morning.

Every machine described in the front of the book has a timed baking cycle that allows you to fill and set the machine the night before and to wake to freshly baked bread. For this alone, bread machines are worthwhile.

Stocking your pantry with grains and dried fruits gives you so many possibilities. You can wake up to Bran and Sour Cherry Bread one morning and Amaranth and Dried Apple Bread the next. With the dough waiting for you, you can bake bagels and buns before you are out of your robe and slippers.

When invited to weekend brunch, bring a bread. For a holiday breakfast, feature Cranberry Buns and Banana Raisin Bread. Who will ever miss the eggs and bacon? On a camping trip, carry Apple Raisin Bread or Morning Mocha Bread to nibble at sunrise.

Apple Raisin Bread

This breakfast bread, full of sweetness and flavor, can make a morning beautiful. But do not begin it on a timed setting the night before, since the oats may absorb water and make the bread very heavy. If you want to prepare Apple Raisin Bread ahead, bake it on the simplest bread cycle the evening before, and let it cool overnight.

SMALL LOAF (1 POUND)	INGREDIENTS	LARGE LOAF (1½ POUNDS)
1½ teaspoons	dry yeast	2¼ teaspoons
1¼ cups	bread flour	2 cups
1 cup	whole wheat flour	1½ cups
¼ cup	rolled oats	⅓ cup
½ teaspoon	salt	¾ teaspoon
½ cup	apple butter (no sugar added)	¾ cup
⅔ cup	water	1 cup
¼ cup	raisins	⅓ cup

1. Add all ingredients except the raisins in the order suggested by your bread machine manual and process on the basic bread cycle according to the manufacturer's directions.

2. Add the raisins at the beeper or at the end of the first kneading in machines without a beeper to signal addition of fruit and nuts.

PER (1-OUNCE) SERVING: 93 Calories; .42 gm. Fat; 0 mg. Cholesterol; 4% Calories from Fat

Cranberry Buns

A luscious picture of cranberry upside-down muffins in Susan G. Purdy's Have Your Cake and Eat It, Too *inspired these ruby-topped buns, festive enough for Thanksgiving or Christmas morning.*

Yield: 12 buns, 12 servings

DOUGH	INGREDIENTS
1½ teaspoons	dry yeast
1¼ cups	bread flour
1 cup	whole wheat flour
½ teaspoon	salt
¼ cup	minced dried figs*
¾ cup plus 2 tablespoons	water

TOPPING	INGREDIENTS
1 cup	apple juice concentrate, thawed
1½ cups	fresh cranberries
1 cup	raisins
	Vegetable cooking spray

1. Add all ingredients for the dough in the order suggested by your bread machine manual and process on the dough cycle according to the manufacturer's directions.
2. While the dough is being processed, prepare the topping: Bring the apple juice concentrate to a boil in a medium nonreactive saucepan. Boil over medium heat 5 minutes, or until reduced by half. Add the cranberries and raisins and remove

from the heat. Coat 12 muffin cups with vegetable cooking spray. Divide the cranberry topping among the cups. Let cool.

3. Preheat the oven to 350 degrees. When the dough cycle ends, remove the dough from the machine and divide into 12 pieces. Roll each into a ball and place on top of the cranberry mixture in a muffin cup. Cover the dough and let rise in a draft-free place 20 minutes, or until doubled.

4. Bake 20 minutes. Invert muffin tin onto a large tray. Cool at least 10 minutes.

*If the figs are hard, pour boiling water over them to soften, then drain well.

PER SERVING: 182 Calories; 1 gm. Fat; 41 mg. Cholesterol; 5% Calories from Fat

---

Whole Wheat Raisin Bagels

The bagel dough can be prepared the night before, covered, and refrigerated. In the morning, boil and bake the bagels and enjoy them warm, sliced and smeared with yogurt cheese.

Yield: 8 bagels, 8 servings

---

2 teaspoons	dry yeast
1¼ cups	bread flour
1 cup	whole wheat flour
½ teaspoon	salt
2 teaspoons	apple juice concentrate, thawed
½ cup	raisins
¾ cup plus 2 tablespoons	water
1 tablespoon	barley malt syrup (optional)*

1. Add all ingredients for the dough except the barley malt syrup in the order suggested by your bread machine manual and process on the dough cycle according to the manufacturer's directions.

2. At the end of the dough cycle, remove the dough from the machine. Preheat the oven to 350 degrees. In a large pot, bring 2 quarts of water to a boil.

3. While the water comes to a boil, divide the dough into 8 equal pieces. Roll each piece into a rope 12 inches long. Make a circle of each piece, overlapping the ends by at least 1 inch and pressing or rolling the overlap tightly to seal. Let the bagels rest for 5 minutes.

4. Add the malt syrup, if using, to the boiling water. (The syrup gives the bagels a golden crust.) Lower a few bagels at a time into the boiling water. As soon as the bagels rise to the top, remove with a skimmer or spatula to a nonstick baking sheet. Bake 15 minutes, or until golden.

*Barley malt syrup is available at some health food stores or by mail order from sources listed on page 12. If it is omitted, the bagels will be lighter in color, but the flavor will be almost the same.

PER SERVING: 164 Calories; 1 gm. Fat; 0 mg. Cholesterol; 4% Calories from Fat

---

Onion Wheatberry Bagels

This bagel has enough flavor and texture to make it on its own for breakfast or a snack. Sliced thin and toasted, it tastes great with wine or juice spritzers.

Yield: 8 bagels, 8 servings

1 tablespoon	dry yeast
2 cups	bread flour
2 tablespoons	wheat bran
1 tablespoon	dried onion flakes
½ teaspoon	salt
¼ cup	cooked wheatberries (see page 5)
¾ cup plus 1 tablespoon	water
1 tablespoon	barley malt syrup (optional)*

1. Add all ingredients except the barley malt syrup in the order suggested by your bread machine manual and process on the dough cycle according to the manufacturer's directions.

2. At the end of the dough cycle, remove the dough from the machine. Preheat the oven to 375 degrees. In a large pot, bring 2 quarts of water to a boil.

3. While the water comes to a boil, divide the dough into 8 equal pieces. Roll each piece into a rope 12 inches long. Make a circle of each piece, overlapping the ends by at least 1 inch and pressing or rolling the overlap tightly to seal. Let the bagels rest 5 minutes.

4. Add the malt syrup, if using, to the boiling water. (The syrup gives the bagels a golden crust.) Lower a few bagels at a time into the boiling water. As soon as the bagels rise to the top, remove with a skimmer or spatula to a nonstick baking sheet. Bake 15 minutes, or until golden.

*Barley malt syrup is available at some health food stores or by mail order from sources listed on page 12. If it is omitted, the bagels will be lighter in color, but the flavor will be almost the same.

PER SERVING: 142 Calories; .9 gm. Fat; 0 mg. Cholesterol; 6% Calories from Fat

Amaranth and Dried Apple Bread

Eating this barely sweet bread for breakfast will boost your protein for the day. The grain highest in protein is amaranth.

SMALL LOAF (1 POUND)	INGREDIENTS	LARGE LOAF (1½ POUNDS)
½ cup	water	¾ cup
¼ cup	amaranth grain	⅓ cup
¼ cup	chopped dried apples or dried pears	⅓ cup
1¼ teaspoons	dry yeast	2 teaspoons
2 cups	bread flour	3 cups
2 tablespoons	wheat bran	3 tablespoons
2 tablespoons	nonfat dry milk	3 tablespoons
½ teaspoon	salt	¾ teaspoon
¾ cup	water	1 cup

1. Bring ½ (¾) cup of water to a boil. Add the amaranth, stir, and return to a boil. Simmer 10 minutes, drain, and let cool to room temperature.

2. Add all ingredients including the cooled amaranth in the order suggested by your bread machine manual and process on the basic bread cycle according to the manufacturer's directions.

PER (1-OUNCE) SERVING: 80 Calories; .5 gm. Fat; .1 mg. Cholesterol; 6% Calories From fat

Double Apple Bread

Because of the naturally sweet taste and mild flavor of the spices, this bread is a favorite among children. The first bite says "apple pie" to your taste buds. But it is not too sweet for breakfast, especially with yogurt cheese or low-fat cream cheese on top.

SMALL LOAF (1 POUND)	INGREDIENTS	LARGE LOAF (1½ POUNDS)
1 teaspoon	dry yeast	1½ teaspoons
1¾ cups	bread flour	2⅔ cups
½ cup	whole wheat flour	¾ cup
1 teaspoon	ground cinnamon	1½ teaspoons
½ teaspoon	grated nutmeg	¾ teaspoon
½ teaspoon	ground cloves	¾ teaspoon
½ teaspoon	salt	¾ teaspoon
¼ cup	apple juice concentrate, thawed	⅓ cup
⅔ cup	water	1 cup
½ cup	chopped unsweetened dried apples	¾ cup

1. Add all ingredients except the dried apples according to your bread machine manual and process according to the manufacturer's directions.

2. Add the apples at the beeper or at the end of the first kneading in machines without a beeper to signal addition of fruit and nuts.

PER (1-OUNCE) SERVING: 82 Calories; .4 gm. Fat; 0 mg. Cholesterol; 4% Calories from Fat

Banana Buttermilk Bread

This brunch or afternoon tea bread is laced with the delicate flavor, sweetness, and texture of banana. Buttermilk adds richness with little fat. Or eat it at sunrise with hot chocolate or Champagne.

SMALL LOAF (1 POUND)	INGREDIENTS	LARGE LOAF (1½ POUNDS)
1 teaspoon	dry yeast	1½ teaspoons
2 cups	bread flour	3 cups
2 tablespoons	wheat bran	3 tablespoons
½ teaspoon	salt	¾ teaspoon
½ cup	mashed ripe banana	⅔ cup
¼ cup	low-fat buttermilk	⅓ cup
½ cup	water	⅔ cup

Add all ingredients in the order suggested by your bread machine manual and process on the basic bread cycle according to the manufacturer's directions.

PER (1-OUNCE) SERVING: 72 Calories; .4 gm. Fat; .2 mg. Cholesterol; 5% Calories from Fat

Banana Raisin Bread

This is an excellent bread to make on the timer, to fill the bread machine the night before and wake to the smell of banana, raisins, and yeasty bread. Eat it warm—not hot—for an almost buttery taste.

SMALL LOAF (1 POUND)	INGREDIENTS	LARGE LOAF (1½ POUNDS)
1¼ teaspoons	dry yeast	2 teaspoons
1¾ cups	bread flour	2⅔ cups
½ cup	whole wheat flour	¾ cup
½ teaspoon	salt	¾ teaspoon
¼ cup	raisins	⅓ cup
¼ cup	mashed banana	⅓ cup
¾ cup	water	1 cup plus 2 tablespoons

Add all ingredients in the order suggested by your bread machine manual and process on the basic bread cycle according to the manufacturer's directions.

PER (1-OUNCE) SERVING: 78 Calories; .3 gm. Fat; 0 mg. Cholesterol; 4% Calories from Fat

Bran Muffin Bread

This loaf is excellent at breakfast, especially for bran muffin lovers. Prunes and raisins not only sweeten the bread, but, along with the bran, make it rich in fiber.

SMALL LOAF (1 POUND)	INGREDIENTS	LARGE LOAF (1½ POUNDS)
1 teaspoon	dry yeast	1½ teaspoons
1½ cups	bread flour	2¼ cups
½ cup	whole wheat flour	¾ cup
½ cup	wheat bran	¾ cup
½ teaspoon	salt	¾ teaspoon
2 tablespoons	minced prunes*	3 tablespoons
1	egg white(s)	2
⅔ cup	water	1 cup
½ cup	raisins	¾ cup

1. Add all ingredients except the raisins in the order suggested by your bread machine manual and process on the basic bread cycle according to the manufacturer's directions.

2. Add the raisins at the beeper or at the end of the first kneading in machines without a beeper to signal addition of fruit and nuts.

*If the prunes are hard, pour boiling water over them to soften, then drain well.

PER (1-OUNCE) SERVING: 81 Calories; .4 gm. Fat; 0 mg. Cholesterol; 4% Calories from Fat

Bran and Sour Cherry Bread

Dried sour cherries give this high, light bread a fruity, slightly tart taste just right for breakfast. It doesn't even need butter, and it makes a great snack. If you plan to stuff a goose, use this bread.

SMALL LOAF (1 POUND)	INGREDIENTS	LARGE LOAF (1½ POUNDS)
1 teaspoon	dry yeast	1½ teaspoons
2 cups	bread flour	3 cups
¼ cup	wheat bran	⅓ cup
2 tablespoons	nonfat dry milk	3 tablespoons
Pinch of	ground cloves	⅛ teaspoon
½ teaspoon	salt	¾ teaspoon
¾ cup plus 2 tablespoons	water	1¼ cups
½ cup	dried sour cherries	¾ cup

1. Add all ingredients except the dried cherries in the order suggested by your bread machine manual and process on the basic bread cycle according to the manufacturer's directions.

2. Add the dried cherries at the beeper or at the end of the first kneading in machines without a beeper to signal addition of fruit and nuts.

PER (1-OUNCE) SERVING: 77 Calories; .3 gm. Fat; .1 mg. Cholesterol; 4% Calories from Fat

Sweet Buckwheat Bread

Start the day with this fruited bread, so rich in taste and texture yet meager in fat. It is just as good later in the day with tea or hot chocolate.

SMALL LOAF (1 POUND)	INGREDIENTS	LARGE LOAF (1½ POUNDS)
¼ cup	buckwheat groats (kasha)	⅓ cup
¼ cup	water	⅓ cup
1½ teaspoons	dry yeast	2¼ teaspoons
2 cups	bread flour	3 cups
2 tablespoons	nonfat dry milk	3 tablespoons
2 tablespoons	minced prunes*	3 tablespoons
½ teaspoon	salt	¾ teaspoon
¾ cup plus 2 tablespoons	water	1¼ cups
¼ cup	raisins	⅓ cup

1. Simmer groats in ¼ (⅓) cup water until water is absorbed, about 5 minutes. Let cool.

2. Add groats and all remaining ingredients except the raisins in the order suggested by your bread machine manual and process on the basic bread cycle according to the manufacturer's directions.

3. Add the raisins at the beeper or at the end of the first kneading in machines without a beeper to signal addition of fruit and nuts.

*If the prunes are hard, pour boiling water over them to soften, then drain well.

PER (1-OUNCE) SERVING: 83 Calories; .4 gm. Fat; .1 mg. Cholesterol; 4% Calories from Fat

Carrot and Ginger Bread

If you want to sell your home, make this bread when prospective buyers visit. Its spicy fragrance permeates any house or apartment. Have it for breakfast, plain or toasted.

SMALL LOAF (1 POUND)	INGREDIENTS	LARGE LOAF (1½ POUNDS)
1 teaspoon	dry yeast	1½ teaspoons
1¾ cups	bread flour	2⅔ cups
½ cup	whole wheat flour	¾ cup
2 tablespoons	nonfat dry milk	3 tablespoons
1 teaspoon	apple butter	1½ teaspoons
1 teaspoon	ground ginger	1½ teaspoons
½ teaspoon	ground cinnamon	¾ teaspoon
¼ teaspoon	ground cloves	½ teaspoon
½ teaspoon	salt	¾ teaspoon
2 tablespoons	minced dried figs or prunes*	3 tablespoons
⅓ cup	grated carrots	½ cup
¾ cup	water	1 cup

Add all ingredients in the order suggested by your bread machine manual and process on the basic bread cycle according to the manufacturer's directions.

*If the figs or prunes are hard, pour boiling water over them to soften, then drain well.

PER (1-OUNCE) SERVING: 75 Calories; .3 gm. Fat; .1 mg. Cholesterol; 4% Calories from Fat

Cherries and Yogurt Bread

Children will especially like this mildly tart, sweetly spiced bread. Serve it for breakfast with yogurt and toasted oats on top. Or take it to the beach and watch the sun rise.

SMALL LOAF (1 POUND)	INGREDIENTS	LARGE LOAF (1½ POUNDS)
½ cup	nonfat plain yogurt	¾ cup
1¼ teaspoons	dry yeast	2 teaspoons
1½ cups	bread flour	2¼ cups
¾ cup	whole wheat flour	1 cup plus 2 tablespoons
1 teaspoon	ground cinnamon	1½ teaspoons
¼ teaspoon	ground cloves	½ teaspoon
½ teaspoon	salt	¾ teaspoon
2 tablespoons	minced prunes*	3 tablespoons
1	egg white(s)	2
⅓ cup	water	½ cup
½ cup	dried cherries	¾ cup

1. Drain yogurt in a cheesecloth or a coffee filter at least 1 hour.
2. Add all ingredients including the drained yogurt in the order suggested by your bread machine manual and process on the basic bread cycle according to the manufacturer's directions.

*If the prunes are hard, pour boiling water over them to soften, then drain well.

PER (1-OUNCE) SERVING: 85 Calories; .3 gm. Fat; .1 mg. Cholesterol; 4% Calories from Fat

Cinnamon-Raisin Bread

This bread is mildly sweet, gently spiced, soft, and moist. It is rich in fiber, potassium, and iron.

SMALL LOAF (1 POUND)	INGREDIENTS	LARGE LOAF (1½ POUNDS)
1¼ teaspoons	dry yeast	1¾ teaspoons
1¾ cups	bread flour	2⅔ cups
½ cup	whole wheat flour	¾ cup
2 tablespoons	nonfat dry milk	3 tablespoons
½ teaspoon	ground cinnamon	¾ teaspoon
¼ teaspoon	ground cloves	½ teaspoon
½ cup	mashed banana	¾ cup
½ teaspoon	salt	¾ teaspoon
½ cup	water	¾ cup
½ cup	raisins	¾ cup

1. Add all ingredients except the raisins in the order suggested by your bread machine manual and process on the basic bread cycle according to the manufacturer's directions.

2. Add the raisins at the beeper or at the end of the first kneading in machines without a beeper to signal addition of fruit and nuts.

PER (1-OUNCE) SERVING: 90 Calories; .4 gm. Fat; .1 mg. Cholesterol; 4% Calories from Fat

Cranberry and Oat Bread

From October to December, when cranberries brighten fruit stands, this light, fruity bread can start your day or liven it up in the afternoon beside hot chocolate or tea.

SMALL LOAF (1 POUND)	INGREDIENTS	LARGE LOAF (1½ POUNDS)
1¼ teaspoons	dry yeast	2¼ teaspoons
2 cups	bread flour	3 cups
¼ cup	rolled oats	⅓ cup
2 tablespoons	nonfat dry milk	3 tablespoons
¼ cup	wheat bran	⅓ cup
1 tablespoon	grated orange zest	1½ tablespoons
½ teaspoon	salt	¾ teaspoon
½ cup	fresh cranberries	¾ cup
¾ cup	water	1 cup

Add all ingredients in the order suggested by your bread machine manual and process on the basic bread cycle according to the manufacturer's directions.

PER (1-OUNCE) SERVING: 74 Calories; .4 gm. Fat; .1 mg. Cholesterol; 5% Calories from Fat

Date, Orange, and Wheatberry Bread

This soft, fruity bread with the crunch of wheatberries tastes great in the morning or for an after-school snack.

SMALL LOAF (1 POUND)	INGREDIENTS	LARGE LOAF (1½ POUNDS)
1¼ teaspoons	dry yeast	2 teaspoons
1¾ cups	bread flour	2⅔ cups
½ cup	whole wheat flour	¾ cup
2 tablespoons	nonfat dry milk	3 tablespoons
2 teaspoons	grated orange zest	1 tablespoon
½ teaspoon	salt	¾ teaspoon
¼ cup	chopped dates	⅓ cup
¼ cup	cooked wheatberries (see page 5)	½ cup
1	egg white(s)	2
⅔ cup	water	¾ cup plus 2 tablespoons

Add all ingredients in the order suggested by your bread machine manual and process on the basic bread cycle according to the manufacturer's directions.

PER (1-OUNCE) SERVING: 83 Calories; .4 gm. Fat; .1 mg. Cholesterol; 4% Calories from Fat

Morning Mocha Bread

Here is a particularly good bread to make on the timed cycle and have waiting for you fresh, warm, and fragrant in the morning. Spread with yogurt cheese or low-fat cottage cheese and top with a very light dusting of cinnamon or cocoa.

SMALL LOAF (1 POUND)	INGREDIENTS	LARGE LOAF (1½ POUNDS)
1½ teaspoons	dry yeast	2¼ teaspoons
1¾ cups	bread flour	2⅔ cups
½ cup	rye flour	¾ cup
2 tablespoons	unsweetened cocoa powder	3 tablespoons
¾ teaspoon	salt	1 teaspoon
2 tablespoons	minced prunes*	3 tablespoons
¾ cup plus 2 tablespoons	strong brewed coffee, cooled to room temperature	1¼ cups

Add all ingredients in the order suggested by your bread machine manual and process on the basic bread cycle according to the manufacturer's directions.

*If the prunes are hard, pour boiling water over them to soften, then drain well.

PER (1-OUNCE) SERVING: 73 Calories; .4 gm. Fat; 0 mg. Cholesterol; 5% Calories from Fat

Oat and Raisin Bread

This bread tastes sweet enough to serve as a coffee cake. If you want it even sweeter, spread with mashed ripe banana or mango.

SMALL LOAF (1 POUND)	INGREDIENTS	LARGE LOAF (1½ POUNDS)
1 teaspoon	dry yeast	1½ teaspoons
2 cups	bread flour	3 cups
¼ cup	rolled oats	⅓ cup
½ teaspoon	ground cinnamon	¾ teaspoon
½ teaspoon	salt	¾ teaspoon
2 tablespoons	apple butter (no sugar added)	3 tablespoons
¾ cup plus 2 tablespoons	water	1⅓ cups
¼ cup	raisins	⅓ cup

1. Add all ingredients except the raisins in the order suggested by your bread machine manual and process on the basic bread cycle according to the manufacturer's directions.

2. Add the raisins at the beeper or at the end of the first kneading in machines without a beeper to signal addition of fruit and nuts.

PER (1-OUNCE) SERVING: 81 Calories; .4 gm. Fat; 0 mg. Cholesterol; 4% Calories from Fat

Pineapple and Sweet Potato Bread

This bread is sweet, but not too sweet for breakfast. Slicing it thick and toasting it under a broiler or in a toaster oven will caramelize the pineapple and intensify the sweetness for a treat later in the day.

SMALL LOAF (1 POUND)	INGREDIENTS	LARGE LOAF (1½ POUNDS)
1 teaspoon	dry yeast	1½ teaspoons
1¾ cups	bread flour	2⅔ cups
½ cup	whole wheat flour	¾ cup
2 tablespoons	nonfat dry milk	3 tablespoons
½ teaspoon	salt	¾ teaspoon
½ cup	mashed sweet potato	¾ cup
½ cup	water	⅔ cup
½ cup	fresh or drained unsweetened canned pineapple chunks (½-inch)	¾ cup

1. Add all the ingredients except the pineapple chunks in the order suggested by your bread machine manual and process on the basic bread cycle according to the manufacturer's directions.

2. Add the pineapple at the beeper or at the end of the first kneading in machines without a beeper to signal addition of fruit and nuts.

PER (1-OUNCE) SERVING: 83 Calories; .4 gm. Fat; .1 mg. Cholesterol; 4% Calories from Fat

Raisin Pumpernickel

SMALL LOAF (1 POUND)	INGREDIENTS	LARGE LOAF (1½ POUNDS)
1 teaspoon	dry yeast	1½ teaspoons
2 cups	bread flour	3 cups
½ cup	rye flour	¾ cup
1 teaspoon	caraway seeds	1½ teaspoons
½ teaspoon	salt	¾ teaspoon
2 teaspoons	caramel coloring (optional)*	1 tablespoon
⅓ cup	sourdough starter**	½ cup
⅔ cup	water	1 cup
1 cup	raisins	1½ cups

1. Add all ingredients except the raisins in the order suggested by your bread machine manual and process on the basic bread cycle according to the manufacturer's directions.

2. Add the raisins at the beeper or at the end of the first kneading in machines without a beeper to signal addition of fruit and nuts.

*See mail-order sources on page 12. If the caramel coloring is omitted, the bread will be lighter in color, but the flavor will be the same.

**After measuring out what is needed for this recipe, be sure to replenish your sourdough starter with equal amounts of flour and water.

PER (1-OUNCE) SERVING: 106 Calories; .4 gm. Fat; 0 mg. Cholesterol, 3% Calories from Fat

Scandinavian Bread with Raisins

The scent and flavor of cardamom evoke thoughts of Danish pastries. Yet this is neither very sweet nor rich, but an every morning bread to eat toasted or plain spread with mashed ripe fruit or nonfat yogurt cheese.

SMALL LOAF (1 POUND)	INGREDIENTS	LARGE LOAF (1½ POUNDS)
½ cup	raisins	¾ cup
1¼ teaspoons	dry yeast	2 teaspoons
2 cups	bread flour	3 cups
1 tablespoon	wheat germ	1½ tablespoons
2 tablespoons	wheat bran	3 tablespoons
2 tablespoons	nonfat dry milk	3 tablespoons
½ teaspoon	ground cardamom	¾ teaspoon
¾ teaspoon	salt	1 teaspoon
1	egg white(s)	2
¾ cup	water	1 cup

1. Place the raisins in the colander. Pour boiling water over them. Drain the raisins and let stand until cooled to room temperature.

2. Add all ingredients except the raisins in the order suggested by your bread machine manual and process on the basic bread cycle according to the manufacturer's directions.

3. Add the raisins at the beeper or at the end of the first kneading in machines without a beeper to signal addition of fruit and nuts.

PER (1-OUNCE) SERVING: 82 Calories; .4 gm. Fat; .1 mg. Cholesterol; 4% Calories from Fat

Raisin and Zucchini Bread

For breakfast or tea, even for a chicken salad sandwich, this bread is light in flavor, but rich in vitamins and minerals.

SMALL LOAF (1 POUND)	INGREDIENTS	LARGE LOAF (1½ POUNDS)
1¼ teaspoons	dry yeast	2 teaspoons
1½ cups	bread flour	2¼ cups
¾ cup	whole wheat flour	1 cup plus 2 tablespoons
2 tablespoons	nonfat dry milk	3 tablespoons
¼ teaspoon	ground cloves	½ teaspoon
1 teaspoon	ground cinnamon	1½ teaspoons
½ teaspoon	salt	¾ teaspoon
¼ cup	mashed banana	⅓ cup
½ cup	shredded zucchini	¾ cup
½ cup	water	¾ cup
½ cup	raisins	¾ cup

1. Add all ingredients except the raisins in the order suggested by your bread machine manual and process on the basic bread cycle according to the manufacturer's directions.

2. Add the raisins at the beeper or at the end of the first kneading in machines without a beeper to signal addition of fruit and nuts.

PER (1-OUNCE) SERVING: 86 Calories; .35 gm. Fat; .1 mg. Cholesterol; 4% Calories from Fat

Semolina Bread with Dried Cherries

Semolina flour gives this bread a rustic texture and golden color. Dried cherries make it both tart and sweet. Spread with yogurt cheese and a sprinkle of wheat germ.

SMALL LOAF (1 POUND)	INGREDIENTS	LARGE LOAF (1½ POUNDS)
1¼ teaspoons	dry yeast	2 teaspoons
1¼ cups	bread flour	1¾ cups plus 2 tablespoons
1 cup	semolina flour	1½ cups
2 tablespoons	nonfat dry milk	3 tablespoons
½ teaspoon	salt	¾ teaspoon
1 tablespoon	apple butter (no sugar added)	1½ tablespoons
¾ cup plus 2 tablespoons	water	1¼ cups
½ cup	dried cherries	¾ cup

1. Add all ingredients except the dried cherries in the order suggested by your bread machine manual and process on the basic bread cycle according to the manufacturer's directions.
2. Add the cherries at the beeper or at the end of the first kneading in machines without a beeper to signal addition of fruit and nuts.

PER (1-OUNCE) SERVING: 91 Calories; .3 gm. Fat; .1 mg. Cholesterol; 3% Calories from Fat

Fruited Zucchini Bread

When you want something different but not weird for breakfast, serve this bread, filled with so many good, sweet things that it needs no spread or toasting.

SMALL LOAF (1 POUND)	INGREDIENTS	LARGE LOAF (1½ POUNDS)
1 teaspoon	dry yeast	1½ teaspoons
1¾ cups	bread flour	2⅔ cups
½ cup	whole wheat flour	¾ cup
½ teaspoon	salt	¾ teaspoon
2 tablespoons	minced prunes*	3 tablespoons
⅓ cup	low-fat buttermilk	½ cup
1 cup	grated zucchini	1½ cups
¼ cup	water	⅓ cup
¼ cup	chopped unsweetened dried apples	⅓ cup

1. Add all ingredients except the apples in the order suggested by your bread machine manual and process according to the manufacturer's directions.

2. Add the apples at the beeper or at the end of the first kneading in machines without a beeper to signal addition of fruit and nuts.

*If the prunes are hard, pour boiling water over them to soften, then drain well.

PER (1-OUNCE) SERVING: 77 Calories; .37 gm. Fat; .20 mg. Cholesterol; 4% Calories from Fat

Chapter Two
Sandwich Breads

Better bread—fresher, more aromatic, chewier, and with more layers of texture—needs a smaller amount of filling to make a great sandwich. The low-fat, sugar-free sandwich breads in this chapter are firm textured and are made to be filled. They will not overpower their filling, but will add their flavor to the total savor of the sandwich. Bread becomes the co-star rather than a bit player in the sandwich scene.

By association, the earthy taste of Onion and Potato Bread conveys the illusion that there is meat even if you don't use any or add only a see-through-thin slice. The Whole Wheat Baguettes and Five- or Seven-Grain Breads have enough character to make a hearty lunch when filled with crisp raw or grilled vegetables. Beer Bread and Black Bread both support elegant open-faced sandwiches that can be imaginatively decorated for lunch or a late-night buffet.

Of course, all the breads in this chapter slice especially well, and they make excellent toast. Yesterday's bread for tuna or lettuce and tomato sandwiches can make a great crouton with today's soup or stew. To vary the condiments of your sandwiches and reduce fat even further, instead of butter or mayonnaise, try bread spread with pureed sun-dried tomatoes or roasted garlic.

Layer Black Bread and fillings to make a torta. Slice into wedges or squares, fasten with a toothpick, and have a sandwich party. Or slip a slice of pear or apple between slices of Buttermilk Corn Bread or Green Apple and Curry Bread to make a sandwich for one.

Green Apple and Curry Bread

This sandwich bread has just enough flavor to jazz up tuna or turkey without dominating the combination.

SMALL LOAF (1 POUND)	INGREDIENTS	LARGE LOAF (1½ POUNDS)
1¼ teaspoons	dry yeast	2 teaspoons
2 cups	bread flour	3 cups
2 tablespoons	wheat bran	3 tablespoons
2 tablespoons	rolled oats	3 tablespoons
2 tablespoons	nonfat dry milk	3 tablespoons
1 teaspoon	curry powder	1½ teaspoons
½ teaspoon	salt	¾ teaspoon
¼ cup	chopped green apple (including skin)	⅓ cup
⅔ cup	water	1 cup

Add all ingredients in the order suggested by your bread machine manual and process on the basic bread cycle according to the manufacturer's directions.

PER (1-OUNCE) SERVING: 72 Calories; .4 gm. Fat; .1 mg. Cholesterol; 5% Calories from Fat

Barley and Potato Bread with Thyme

Barley adds toasty flavor and variety to the texture of this moist, soft bread. Fill with cold salmon or sardines, with raw spinach and chopped egg whites, or with cold meats and mustard.

SMALL LOAF (1 POUND)	INGREDIENTS	LARGE LOAF (1½ POUNDS)
1 teaspoon	dry yeast	1½ teaspoons
1¾ cups	bread flour	2⅔ cups
½ cup	whole wheat flour	¾ cup
¼ cup	barley flakes*	⅓ cup
½ cup	mashed potato	¾ cup
½ teaspoon	salt	¾ teaspoon
1 teaspoon	dried thyme leaves	1½ teaspoons
⅓ cup	low-fat buttermilk	½ cup
¼ cup	water	¼ cup plus 2 tablespoons

Add all ingredients in the order suggested by your bread machine manual and process on the basic bread cycle according to the manufacturer's directions.

*Barley flakes are available at health food stores.

PER (1-OUNCE) SERVING: 81 Calories; .4 gm. Fat; .2 mg. Cholesterol; 4% Calories from Fat

Beer Bread

Leftover or flat beer is fine for this mellow sandwich bread, which I like to fill with Waldorf salad (apple chunks, raisins, walnuts, and low-fat mayonnaise) or with tuna or cold meat.

SMALL LOAF (1 POUND)	INGREDIENTS	LARGE LOAF (1½ POUNDS)
1 teaspoon	dry yeast	1½ teaspoons
2 cups	bread flour	3 cups
¼ cup	rye flour	⅓ cup
2 tablespoons	minced dried figs or prunes*	3 tablespoons
½ teaspoon	salt	¾ teaspoon
½ cup	beer	¾ cup
½ cup	water	⅔ cup

Add all ingredients in the order suggested by your bread machine manual and process on the basic bread cycle according to the manufacturer's directions.

*If the figs or prunes are hard, pour boiling water over them to soften, then drain well.

PER (1-OUNCE) SERVING: 75 Calories; .3 gm. Fat; 0 mg. Cholesterol; 4% Calories from Fat

Black Bread

This dense pumpernickel is best sliced thin and used as a base for canapés. Cover with smoked salmon or pickled vegetables and the whites of hard-boiled eggs.

SMALL LOAF (1 POUND)	INGREDIENTS	LARGE LOAF (1½ POUNDS)
1¼ teaspoons	dry yeast	1¾ teaspoons
1¼ cups	bread flour	2 cups
¾ cup	whole wheat flour	1 cup plus 2 tablespoons
½ cup	rye flour	¾ cup
½ teaspoon	salt	¾ teaspoon
¼ cup	minced prunes*	⅓ cup
1 teaspoon	caramel coloring (optional)**	1½ teaspoons
½ cup	sourdough starter***	¾ cup
⅔ cup	water	1 cup

Add all ingredients in the order suggested by your bread machine manual and process on the basic bread cycle according to the manufacturer's directions.

*If the prunes are hard, pour boiling water over them to soften, then drain well.
**Mail-order sources for caramel coloring are on page 12. If it is omitted, the bread will be lighter in color, but the flavor will be the same.
***After measuring out what is needed for this recipe, be sure to replenish your sourdough starter with equal amounts of flour and water.

PER (1-OUNCE) SERVING: 83 Calories; .4 gm. Fat; 0 mg. Cholesterol; 4% Calories from Fat

Boston Brown Bread

Like Boston baked beans, this bread contains mustard and spice, but figs and soy sauce substitute for molasses, making the mahogany loaf just barely sweet and very moist. Cut it into thin slices for open-faced sandwiches of turkey with curried yogurt or sliced radishes, cucumber, and scallions.

SMALL LOAF (1 POUND)	INGREDIENTS	LARGE LOAF (1½ POUNDS)
1¼ teaspoons	dry yeast	2 teaspoons
1¾ cups	bread flour	2⅔ cups
½ cup	whole wheat flour	¾ cup
½ teaspoon	ground cloves	¾ teaspoon
1 teaspoon	soy sauce	1½ teaspoons
2 tablespoons	Dijon-style mustard	3 tablespoons
¼ cup	minced dried figs*	⅓ cup
¾ cup	water	1 cup plus 2 tablespoons

Add all ingredients in the order suggested by your bread machine manual and process on the basic bread cycle according to the manufacturer's directions.

*If the figs are hard, pour boiling water over them to soften, then drain well.

PER (1-OUNCE) SERVING: 78 Calories; .5 gm. Fat; 0 mg. Cholesterol; 6% Calories from Fat

Cocoa Bread

This bread is just positive enough on the sweetness scale to appeal to children. Snack on brown bread covered with thinly sliced pears or fill it with smoked turkey and sweet red apple slices.

SMALL LOAF (1 POUND)	INGREDIENTS	LARGE LOAF (1½ POUNDS)
1¼ teaspoons	dry yeast	2 teaspoons
2 cups	bread flour	3 cups
½ cup	mashed potato	¾ cup
¼ cup	wheat bran	⅓ cup
2 tablespoons	nonfat dry milk	3 tablespoons
1 tablespoon	unsweetened cocoa powder	1½ tablespoons
¾ teaspoon	salt	1 teaspoon
⅓ cup	strong coffee (at room temperature)	½ cup
½ cup	water	¾ cup

Add all ingredients in the order suggested by your bread machine manual and process on the basic bread cycle according to the manufacturer's directions.

PER (1-OUNCE) SERVING: 72 Calories; .4 gm. Fat; .1 mg. Cholesterol; 4% Calories from Fat

Buckwheat Bread

This moist, nutty, spicy bread is close grained and not tall. Let it cool completely, then slice thin and fill with crisp radishes, cucumber, and tomato with or without sliced turkey.

SMALL LOAF (1 POUND)	INGREDIENTS	LARGE LOAF (1½ POUNDS)
½ cup	buckwheat groats (kasha)	¾ cup
1½ teaspoons	dry yeast	2¼ teaspoons
2 cups	bread flour	3 cups
2 tablespoons	nonfat dry milk	3 tablespoons
¼ teaspoon	freshly ground black pepper	½ teaspoon
2 teaspoons	dried minced onion	1 tablespoon
¾ teaspoon	salt	1 teaspoon
1 cup	water	1⅓ cups

1. In a nonstick frying pan, toast the buckwheat about 5 minutes, until lightly browned. Shake the pan so the buckwheat does not burn. Toasting increases the flavor.

2. Add all ingredients in the order suggested by your bread machine manual and process on the basic bread cycle according to the manufacturer's directions.

PER (1-OUNCE) SERVING: 83 Calories; .4 gm. Fat; .1 mg. Cholesterol; 5% Calories from Fat

Butternut Squash and Balsamic Vinegar Bread

This is a low bread, which is sweet and flavorful. Slice very thin for tea or thicker to pack in a lunch box.

SMALL LOAF (1 POUND)	INGREDIENTS	LARGE LOAF (1½ POUNDS)
1¼ teaspoons	dry yeast	2 teaspoons
1⅔ cups	bread flour	2½ cups
¾ cup	whole wheat flour	1 cup plus 2 tablespoons
½ teaspoon	salt	¾ teaspoon
¾ cup	mashed baked butternut or acorn squash or canned pumpkin puree	1 cup plus 2 tablespoons
2 tablespoons	balsamic vinegar	3 tablespoons
¼ cup	water	⅓ cup
½ cup	raisins	¾ cup

1. Add all ingredients except the raisins according to your bread machine manual and process on the basic bread cycle according to the manufacturer's directions.
2. Add the raisins at the beeper or at the end of the first kneading in machines without a beeper to signal addition of fruit and nuts.

PER (1-OUNCE) SERVING: 89 Calories; .4 gm. Fat; 0 mg. Cholesterol; 4% Calories from Fat

Carrot and Dill Bread

This light, herbed bread bursting with vitamin C turns into a memorable tuna or chicken salad sandwich. Serve it with split pea, lentil, or other hearty vegetable soups.

SMALL LOAF (1 POUND)	INGREDIENTS	LARGE LOAF (1½ POUNDS)
1 teaspoon	dry yeast	1½ teaspoons
2 cups	bread flour	3 cups
2 tablespoons	rolled oats	3 tablespoons
2 tablespoons	wheat bran	3 tablespoons
2 tablespoons	nonfat dry milk	3 tablespoons
⅓ cup	grated carrots	½ cup
2 tablespoons	minced prunes*	3 tablespoons
1 teaspoon	dried minced onion	1½ teaspoons
2 teaspoons	dried dill weed	1 tablespoon
½ teaspoon	salt	¾ teaspoon
¾ cup	water	1 cup

Add all ingredients in the order suggested by your bread machine manual and process on the basic bread cycle according to the manufacturer's directions.

*If the prunes are hard, pour boiling water over them to soften, then drain well.

PER (1-OUNCE) SERVING: 72 Calories; .3 gm. Fat; .1 mg. Cholesterol; 4% Calories from Fat

Southwestern Carrot Bread

This is a little sweet, a little hot, and just right for grilled chicken or salad greens tossed with ranch dressing. To turn it into a melt, sprinkle sparingly with a full-flavored Cheddar or Jack cheese and broil briefly to melt the cheese.

SMALL LOAF (1 POUND)	INGREDIENTS	LARGE LOAF (1½ POUNDS)
1¼ teaspoons	dry yeast	2 teaspoons
2 cups	bread flour	3 cups
¼ cup	yellow cornmeal	⅓ cup
½ cup	grated carrots	¾ cup
1 teaspoon	ground cumin	1½ teaspoons
⅛ teaspoon	ground cayenne	¼ teaspoon
½ teaspoon	salt	¾ teaspoon
¾ cup	water	1 cup
½ cup	currants or raisins	¾ cup

1. Add all ingredients except the currants in the order suggested by your bread machine manual and process on the basic bread cycle according to the manufacturer's directions.

2. Add the currants at the beeper or at the end of the first kneading in machines without a beeper to signal addition of fruit and nuts.

PER (1-OUNCE) SERVING: 85 Calories; .4 gm. Fat; 0 mg. Cholesterol; 4% Calories from Fat

Low-Fat Challah

Egg yolks and oil or butter traditionally give challah the richness that make it an appropriate celebration bread for the Jewish sabbath. An egg substitute (such as Egg Beaters) and just a drop of saffron or yellow food coloring make this bread a golden, light-textured but still celebratory challah.

SMALL LOAF (1 POUND)	INGREDIENTS	LARGE LOAF (1½ POUNDS)
1½ teaspoons	dry yeast	2¼ teaspoons
¼ cup	water	⅓ cup
¼ cup	apple juice concentrate, thawed	⅓ cup
2 cups	bread flour	3 cups
½ cup	egg substitute	¾ cup
2 tablespoons	apple butter (no sugar added)	3 tablespoons
½ teaspoon	salt	¾ teaspoon
¼ teaspoon	vanilla extract	½ teaspoon
1 teaspoon	grated lemon zest	1½ teaspoons
1 drop	yellow food coloring	2 drops
	or	
2	saffron threads (optional)	3

1. In a medium bowl, dissolve the yeast in the water. Add the apple juice concentrate and 1 cup (1½ cups) of the flour. Stir to form a smooth paste. Cover and let rest in a draft-free place for an hour to form a "sponge."

2. Set aside 1 tablespoon of the egg substitute. Add all the remaining ingredients, in the order suggested by your bread machine manual, adding the sponge with the liquids. Process on the dough cycle according to the manufacturer's directions.

3. When the dough cycle ends, remove the dough from the machine. Preheat the oven to 375 degrees. Divide the dough into 3 equal pieces; it will be sticky. On a floured surface with well-floured hands, roll each piece of dough into a 12(15)-inch-long rope. Braid the pieces into a loaf. Pinch tightly together at each end to seal. Place the challah on a nonstick baking sheet. Brush with the reserved 1 tablespoon egg substitute. Let rise in a draft-free place 30 minutes, or until doubled. **4.** Brush the top of the loaf again very gently with the remaining glaze. Bake 30 minutes, or until golden brown.

PER (1-OUNCE) SERVING: 72 Calories; .3 gm. Fat; 0 mg. Cholesterol; 4% Calories from Fat

Buttermilk Corn Bread

When you serve chili either con carne or vegetarian style, or any spicy stew or salsa, have this soft, barely acidic bread on the side. Or use it for sandwiches with yogurt cheese or cold chicken and salsa.

SMALL LOAF (1 POUND)	INGREDIENTS	LARGE LOAF (1½ POUNDS)
1¼ teaspoons	dry yeast	1¾ teaspoons
1⅔ cups	bread flour	2½ cups
½ cup	yellow cornmeal	¾ cup
2 teaspoons	ground cumin	1 tablespoon
½ teaspoon	salt	¾ teaspoon
Pinch	baking soda	Pinch
2 tablespoons	minced prunes*	3 tablespoons
⅓ cup	low-fat buttermilk	½ cup
⅔ cup	water	¾ cup plus 2 tablespoons

Add all ingredients in the order suggested by your bread machine manual and process on the basic bread cycle according to the manufacturer's directions.

*If the prunes are hard, pour boiling water over them to soften, then drain well.

PER (1-OUNCE) SERVING: 74 Calories; .4 gm. Fat; .2 mg. Cholesterol; 5% Calories from Fat

Corn and Zucchini Bread

Cover a piece of this bread with a slice of tomato and broil. Serve with a chowder or cold soup for lunch.

SMALL LOAF (1 POUND)	INGREDIENTS	LARGE LOAF (1½ POUNDS)
1 teaspoon	dry yeast	1½ teaspoons
1½ cups	bread flour	2¼ cups
¾ cup	whole wheat flour	1 cup plus 2 tablespoons
¼ cup	cooked wheatberries (see page 5)	⅓ cup
Large pinch	cayenne	⅛ teaspoon
2 teaspoons	dried minced onion	1 tablespoon
½ teaspoon	salt	¾ teaspoon
½ cup	grated zucchini	¾ cup
1	egg white(s)	2
⅓ cup	water	½ cup
¼ cup	corn kernels	⅓ cup

1. Add all ingredients except the corn in the order suggested by your bread machine manual and process on the basic bread cycle according to the manufacturer's directions.
2. Add the corn at the beeper or at the end of the first kneading in machines without a beeper to signal addition of fruit and nuts.

PER (1-OUNCE) SERVING: 75 Calories; .4 gm. Fat; 0 mg. Cholesterol; 5% Calories from Fat

Country Bread

This big, round bread starts the day with apple butter or jam and makes excellent sandwiches of any type. By removing the dough from the machine and giving it a long, slow final rise, this recipe will yield a larger-than-usual, rustic-looking bread. Slice it in half horizontally, hollow out the center, and fill with green salad and tomatoes; then drizzle on a little vinaigrette dressing. Weight the top down for about half an hour and slice into wedges.

SMALL LOAF (1 POUND)	INGREDIENTS	LARGE LOAF (1½ POUNDS)
1 teaspoon	dry yeast	1½ teaspoons
1¾ cups	bread flour	2⅔ cups
½ cup	whole wheat flour	¾ cup
¼ cup	rye flour	⅓ cup
½ teaspoon	salt	¾ teaspoon
½ cup	sourdough starter*	¾ cup
⅔ cup	water	1 cup
1 tablespoon	yellow cornmeal	1 tablespoon

1. Add all ingredients except the cornmeal in the order suggested by your bread machine manual and process on the dough cycle according to the manufacturer's directions.

2. At the end of the dough cycle, remove the dough from the machine. Roll between your palms into a ball. Sprinkle a nonstick baking sheet with cornmeal. Put the ball of dough on top, cover loosely, and let rise in a draft-free place about 1 hour, until doubled in size.

3. While the dough is rising, preheat the oven to 375 degrees. When the dough has doubled in size, slash the top with a sharp knife or single-edged razor and bake 45 minutes for dough from the smaller machine and 1 hour for dough from the larger machine. (The dough can also remain in the machine and be baked on the bread cycle.)

*After measuring out what is needed for this recipe, be sure to replenish your sourdough starter with equal amounts of flour and water.

PER (1-OUNCE) SERVING: 82 Calories; .4 gm. Fat; 0 mg. Cholesterol; 4% Calories from Fat

---

Five-Grain Bread

This fiber-rich, moist bread, with a hint of orange, can be sliced thin for tuna, apple and cheese, or peanut butter sandwiches. It makes fragrant breakfast toast.

SMALL LOAF (1 POUND)	INGREDIENTS	LARGE LOAF (1½ POUNDS)
1½ teaspoons	dry yeast	2¼ teaspoons
1½ cups	bread flour	2¼ cups
¼ cup	cooked whole barley	⅓ cup
¼ cup	wheat bran	⅓ cup
¼ cup	yellow cornmeal	⅓ cup
2 tablespoons	rolled oats	3 tablespoons
¼ cup	rye flour	⅓ cup
2 teaspoons	vital wheat gluten*	1 tablespoon
1 tablespoon	grated orange zest	1½ tablespoons
½ teaspoon	salt	¾ teaspoon
¼ cup	minced dried figs**	⅓ cup
1	egg white(s)	2
1 cup	water	1⅓ cups

Add all ingredients in the order suggested by your bread machine manual and process on the basic bread cycle according to the manufacturer's directions.

*Vital wheat gluten is available at health food stores.
**If the figs are hard, pour boiling water over them to soften, then drain well.

PER (1-OUNCE) SERVING: 79 Calories; .4 gm. Fat; 0 mg. Cholesterol; 4% Calories from Fat

Seven-Grain Bread

This multitextured, crunchy bread, packed with fiber, demands an assertive filling, such as salsa and cold chicken, curried tuna, or arugula and cherry tomatoes.

SMALL LOAF (1 POUND)	INGREDIENTS	LARGE LOAF (1½ POUNDS)
1¼ teaspoons	dry yeast	1¾ teaspoons
1¾ cups	bread flour	2⅔ cups
2 tablespoons	cooked buckwheat groats (kasha) (see page 5)	3 tablespoons
2 tablespoons	amaranth grain	3 tablespoons
2 tablespoons	rolled oats	3 tablespoons
2 tablespoons	quinoa grain	3 tablespoons
2 tablespoons	rye flour	3 tablespoons
2 tablespoons	whole wheat flour	3 tablespoons
1 tablespoon	minced prunes*	1½ tablespoons
½ teaspoon	salt	¾ teaspoon
1	egg white(s)	2
¾ cup plus 2 tablespoons	water	1¼ cups

Add all ingredients in the order suggested by your bread machine manual and process on the basic bread cycle according to the manufacturer's directions.

*If the prunes are hard, pour boiling water over them to soften, then drain well.

PER (1-OUNCE) SERVING: 85 Calories; .5 gm. Fat; 0 mg. Cholesterol; 6% Calories from Fat

---

Lentil Bread

Lentils and thyme together are so Mediterranean that they give this bread an evocative taste of faraway places. Tuna without mayo but with sliced tomato and greens between two slices makes a sandwich Niçoise.

SMALL LOAF (1 POUND)	INGREDIENTS	LARGE LOAF (1½ POUNDS)
1¼ teaspoons	dry yeast	2 teaspoons
1¾ cups	bread flour	2⅔ cups
½ cup	whole wheat flour	¾ cup
½ teaspoon	freshly ground black pepper	¾ teaspoon
1 teaspoon	dried thyme leaves	1½ teaspoons
½ teaspoon	salt	¾ teaspoon
¾ cup	cooked lentils	1 cup plus 2 tablespoons
⅔ cup	water	1 cup

Add all ingredients in the order suggested by your bread machine manual and process on the basic bread cycle according to the manufacturer's directions.

PER (1-OUNCE) SERVING: 79 Calories; .4 gm. Fat; 0 mg. Cholesterol; 4% Calories from Fat

Mushroom and Barley Bread

Like my mother's mushroom and barley soup, this bread is rich and flavorful, satisfying without being too filling. Serve with light chicken or vegetable soup or make into a sandwich with sliced pot roast or grilled mushrooms.

SMALL LOAF (1 POUND)	INGREDIENTS	LARGE LOAF (1½ POUNDS)
1¼ teaspoons	dry yeast	2 teaspoons
2 cups	bread flour	3 cups
¼ cup	barley flakes*	⅓ cup
2 tablespoons	wheat bran	3 tablespoons
2 tablespoons	dried minced onions	3 tablespoons
2 tablespoons	crumbled dried imported mushrooms	3 tablespoons
½ teaspoon	salt	¾ teaspoon
¾ cup plus 2 tablespoons	water	1¼ cups

Add all ingredients in the order suggested by your bread machine manual and process on the basic bread cycle according to the manufacturer's directions.

*Barley flakes are available at health food stores.

PER (1-OUNCE) SERVING: 72 Calories; .3 gm. Fat; 0 mg. Cholesterol; 4% Calories from Fat

Onion and Potato Bread

Paired with soup or salad, this light yet crusty bread makes a meal. Fill it with sliced meat, grilled fish, or chicken for a full-flavored sandwich and serve with lemonade or beer.

SMALL LOAF (1 POUND)	INGREDIENTS	LARGE LOAF (1½ POUNDS)
1 teaspoon	dry yeast	1½ teaspoons
2 cups	bread flour	3 cups
½ cup	mashed potato	¾ cup
¼ cup	chopped raw onion	⅓ cup
⅛ teaspoon	freshly ground black pepper	¼ teaspoon
½ teaspoon	salt	¾ teaspoon
¼ cup	sourdough starter*	⅓ cup
½ cup	water	¾ cup

Add all ingredients in the order suggested by your bread machine manual and process on the basic bread cycle according to the manufacturer's directions.

*After measuring out what is needed for this recipe, be sure to replenish your sourdough starter with equal amounts of flour and water.

PER (1-OUNCE) SERVING: 72 Calories; .3 gm. Fat; 0 mg. Cholesterol; 4% Calories from Fat

Pane Rustico

This is Italian country bread, the kind bakers make in villages in the Umbrian hills. It is honest, nourishing, and makes excellent sandwiches. It is also great for mopping up the extra sauce in the bottom of a bowl of pasta.

SMALL LOAF (1 POUND)	INGREDIENTS	LARGE LOAF (1½ POUNDS)
½ cup	cooked wheatberries (see page 5)	⅔ cup
1¼ teaspoons	dry yeast	2 teaspoons
1¼ cups	bread flour	2 cups
1 cup	whole wheat flour	1½ cups
½ teaspoon	salt	¾ teaspoon
⅔ cup	water	1 cup

1. Chop the wheatberries.

2. Add all ingredients in the order suggested by your bread machine manual and process on the basic bread cycle according to the manufacturer's directions.

PER (1-OUNCE) SERVING: 74 Calories; .4 gm. Fat; 0 mg. Cholesterol; 5% Calories from Fat

Herbed Pita Bread

Fill pita with shredded lettuce or other greens, sprouts, chopped tomato, radishes, or anything crisp, and add a little tuna or a few chickpeas for a sensational sandwich. The basil and oregano in the bread mean that salad dressing is not needed for flavor. If the pitas begin to harden before you use them, microwave for 10 seconds to soften.

Yield: 8 pitas, 8 servings

---

2 teaspoons	dry yeast
1¼ cups	bread flour
1 cup	whole wheat flour
2 teaspoons	dried basil
2 teaspoons	dried oregano
½ teaspoon	salt
1 cup	water

1. Add all ingredients in the order suggested by your bread machine manual and process on the dough cycle according to the manufacturer's directions.

2. Preheat the oven to 500 degrees. At the end of the dough cycle divide the dough into 8 equal pieces. On a floured board with floured fingers, press each piece into a circle. Use a floured rolling pin to roll each into a very thin 6-inch circle. Place on nonstick baking sheets. *Do not let rise.* Immediately bake until each pita puffs and browns, 12 to 15 minutes.

PER SERVING: 133 Calories; .7 gm. Fat; 0 mg. Cholesterol; 4% Calories from Fat

Potato and Caraway Bread

Any thick soup plus this hearty loaf makes a whole meal. Cold fish or meat with horseradish-yogurt dressing and cucumber and arugula make fine sandwich fillings for this bread.

SMALL LOAF (1 POUND)	INGREDIENTS	LARGE LOAF (1½ POUNDS)
1¼ teaspoons	dry yeast	2 teaspoons
1½ cups	bread flour	2¼ cups
½ cup	whole wheat flour	¾ cup
¼ cup	wheat bran	⅓ cup
2 tablespoons	nonfat dry milk	3 tablespoons
¼ cup	grated raw potato	⅓ cup
2 teaspoons	caraway seeds	1 tablespoon
½ teaspoon	salt	¾ teaspoon
¾ cup	water	1 cup plus 2 tablespoons

Add all ingredients in the order suggested by your bread machine manual and process on the basic bread cycle according to the manufacturer's directions.

PER (1-OUNCE) SERVING: 67 Calories; 3 gm. Fat; .1 mg. Cholesterol; 5% Calories from Fat

Caraway Hot Dog Rolls

No need to fill these rolls only with hot dogs. Instead, slice them open and fill with salsa and greens or black beans or with Tex-Mex grilled chicken salad, or with grilled peppers and onions.

Yield: 8 rolls, 8 servings

1¼ teaspoons	dry yeast
1¾ cups	bread flour
½ cup	whole wheat flour
1 teaspoon	caraway seeds
2 tablespoons	nonfat dry milk
¾ teaspoon	salt
¾ cup plus 2 tablespoons	water

1. Add all ingredients in the order suggested by your bread machine manual and process on the dough cycle according to the manufacturer's directions.

2. At the end of the dough cycle, remove the dough from the bread machine. Cut into 8 equal pieces. On a floured board with floured hands, roll each piece into a 6-inch-long rope. Place the rolls 3 inches apart on a nonstick baking sheet(s), cover loosely, and let rise in a draft-free place 20 to 30 minutes, until doubled.

3. While the rolls are rising, preheat the oven to 350 degrees. When the rolls have doubled in size, bake until brown, about 20 minutes.

PER ROLL: 140 Calories; .7 gm. Fat; .2 mg. Cholesterol; 4% Calories from Fat

Potato Rolls

Hamburgers and soyburgers taste juicier on these soft buns. If you make the rolls smaller, they are just right for the most elegant dinner.

Yield: 12 rolls, 12 servings   *18 rolls, 18 servings*

SMALL LOAF (1 POUND)	INGREDIENTS	LARGE LOAF (1½ POUNDS)
1¼ teaspoons	dry yeast	2 teaspoons
2 cups	bread flour	3 cups
2 tablespoons	nonfat dry milk	3 tablespoons
2 tablespoons	wheat bran	3 tablespoons
½ cup	mashed potato	¾ cup
½ teaspoon	salt	¾ teaspoon
¾ cup	water	1 cup

1. Add all ingredients for the dough in the order suggested by your bread machine manual and process on the dough cycle according to the manufacturer's directions.
2. At the end of the dough cycle, remove the dough from the machine, divide it into 12 equal pieces (18 pieces in the larger machine). On a floured board with floured hands, roll each piece into a ball. Place the balls 3 inches apart on a nonstick baking sheet(s). Flatten each roll, cover loosely, and let rise in a draft-free place 30 to 40 minutes, until doubled in size.
3. While the bread is rising, preheat the oven to 350 degrees. Bake 20 minutes, or until the rolls are pale golden.

PER SERVING: 94 Calories; .4 gm. Fat; .1 mg. Cholesterol, 4% Calories from Fat

Applesauce Rye Bread

This big-flavored, small-size sandwich bread makes wonderful open-faced sandwiches and canapés. Top with smoked fish or meat or gravlax or marinated artichoke hearts.

SMALL LOAF (1 POUND)	INGREDIENTS	LARGE LOAF (1½ POUNDS)
1½ teaspoons	dry yeast	2¼ teaspoons
1¾ cups	bread flour	2⅔ cups
½ cup	rye flour	¾ cup
2 tablespoons	nonfat dry milk	3 tablespoons
1 teaspoon	grated orange zest	1½ teaspoons
1 teaspoon	aniseed or fennel seed	1½ teaspoons
½ teaspoon	salt	¾ teaspoon
¼ cup	apple butter (no sugar added)	⅓ cup
⅔ cup	water	1 cup

Add all ingredients in the order suggested by your bread machine manual and process on the basic bread cycle according to the manufacturer's directions.

PER (1-OUNCE) SERVING: 71 Calories; .3 gm. Fat; .1 mg. Cholesterol; 4% Calories from Fat

Onion Rye Bread

Here is a finely grained, full-flavored sandwich bread that partners well with sliced tomato and arugula, tuna, roast or corned beef, or low-fat cottage cheese and scallions.

SMALL LOAF (1 POUND)	INGREDIENTS	LARGE LOAF (1½ POUNDS)
¾ cup	minced raw onion	1 cup plus 2 tablespoons
1½ teaspoons	dry yeast	2¼ teaspoons
1¾ cups	bread flour	2⅔ cups
½ cup	rye flour	¾ cup
2 tablespoons	wheat bran	3 tablespoons
½ teaspoon	salt	¾ teaspoon
½ cup plus 1 tablespoon	water	¾ cup plus 1 tablespoon

1. Reserve 1 tablespoon (1½ tablespoons) of minced onion. Add all ingredients except the reserved onion in the order suggested by your bread machine manual and process on the basic bread cycle according to the manufacturer's directions.
2. Pour boiling water over the reserved onion and drain. Early in the final rising period, sprinkle the reserved onion on top of the loaf. Let the bread finish rising and baking in the machine.

PER (1-OUNCE) SERVING: 70 Calories; .3 gm. Fat; 0 mg. Cholesterol; 4% Calories from Fat

Italian Sourdough Bread

This bread is as crusty outside as it is soft and light inside. The herbs give it enough flavor to serve on its own with bouillon or a glass of wine. Or make it into a tomato sandwich.

SMALL LOAF (1 POUND)	INGREDIENTS	LARGE LOAF (1½ POUNDS)
1 teaspoon	dry yeast	1½ teaspoons
2 cups	bread flour	3 cups
½ teaspoon	dried rosemary	¾ teaspoon
½ teaspoon	dried thyme leaves	¾ teaspoon
½ teaspoon	dried oregano	¾ teaspoon
½ teaspoon	dried basil	¾ teaspoon
¼ teaspoon	freshly ground black pepper	½ teaspoon
¾ teaspoon	salt	1 teaspoon
½ cup	sourdough starter*	¾ cup
⅔ cup	water	¾ cup

Add all ingredients in the order suggested by your bread machine manual and process on the basic bread cycle according to the manufacturer's directions.

*After measuring out what is needed for this recipe, be sure to replenish your sourdough starter with equal amounts of flour and water.

PER (1-OUNCE) SERVING: 70 Calories; .3 gm. Fat; 0 Cholesterol; 4% Calories from Fat

Sourdough Rye Bread

SMALL LOAF (1 POUND)	INGREDIENTS	LARGE LOAF (1½ POUNDS)
1½ teaspoons	dry yeast	2¼ teaspoons
1¾ cups	bread flour	2⅔ cups
½ cup	rye flour	¾ cup
2 tablespoons	caraway seeds	3 tablespoons
¾ teaspoon	salt	1 teaspoon
2 teaspoons	barley malt syrup (optional)*	1 tablespoon
¼ cup	sourdough starter**	⅓ cup
⅔ cup	water	1 cup

Add all ingredients in the order suggested by your bread machine manual and process on the basic bread cycle according to the manufacturer's directions.

*Barley malt syrup is available at some health food stores or by mail-order from sources listed on page 12. If it is omitted, the bread will be lighter in color, but the flavor will be almost the same.
**After measuring out what is needed for this recipe, be sure to replenish your sourdough starter with equal amounts of flour and water.

PER (1-OUNCE) SERVING: 73 Calories; .4 gm. Fat; 0 mg. Cholesterol; 5% Calories from Fat

Sourdough Bran and Rye Bread

This hearty sandwich bread is excellent with any filling, from peanut butter and jelly to vegetable pâté, or smoked trout with horseradish dressing (nonfat yogurt mixed with horseradish).

SMALL LOAF (1 POUND)	INGREDIENTS	LARGE LOAF (1½ POUNDS)
1 teaspoon	dry yeast	1½ teaspoons
2 cups	bread flour	3 cups
¼ cup	wheat bran	⅓ cup
¼ cup	rye flour	⅓ cup
½ teaspoon	salt	¾ teaspoon
2 tablespoons	minced prunes*	3 tablespoons
½ cup	sourdough starter**	¾ cup
⅔ cup	water	1 cup

Add all ingredients in the order suggested by your bread machine manual and process on the basic bread cycle according to the manufacturer's directions.

*If the prunes are hard, pour boiling water over them to soften, then drain well.
**After measuring out what is needed for this recipe, be sure to replenish your sourdough starter with equal amounts of flour and water.

PER (1-OUNCE) SERVING: 80 Calories; .4 gm. Fat; 0 mg. Cholesterol; 4% Calories from Fat

Simple Sourdough Bread

With almost any filling, from tuna salad to wild mushroom pâté, sourdough bread makes fine sandwiches or canapés. It is also perfect with everything from spicy sauces to aromatic fish soups like cioppino or gumbo.

SMALL LOAF (1 POUND)	INGREDIENTS	LARGE LOAF (1½ POUNDS)
¾ teaspoon	dry yeast	1¼ teaspoons
1¾ cups	bread flour	2⅔ cups
½ teaspoon	salt	¾ teaspoon
2 tablespoons	wheat bran	3 tablespoons
½ cup	sourdough starter*	¾ cup
⅔ cup	water	1 cup

Add all ingredients in the order suggested by your bread machine manual and process on the basic bread cycle according to the manufacturer's directions.

*After measuring out what is needed for this recipe, be sure to replenish your sourdough starter with equal amounts of flour and water.

PER (1-OUNCE) SERVING: 63 Calories; .3 gm. Fat; 0 mg. Cholesterol; 4% Calories from Fat

Sourdough Dill Bread

We love a certain roadside Connecticut restaurant for serving this dill bread. It wakes you up more gently than a cup of coffee and along with a bowl of soup, fortifies you for your drive. Fill sandwiches with tuna or chicken or cucumber, tomato, and jicama.

SMALL LOAF (1 POUND)	INGREDIENTS	LARGE LOAF (1½ POUNDS)
1 teaspoon	dry yeast	1½ teaspoons
2 cups	bread flour	3 cups
2 tablespoons	wheat bran	3 tablespoons
2 tablespoons	wheat germ	3 tablespoons
1 teaspoon	dried dill weed	1½ teaspoons
1 teaspoon	dill seed	1½ teaspoons
½ teaspoon	salt	¾ teaspoon
¼ cup	mashed banana	⅓ cup
½ cup	sourdough starter*	¾ cup
½ cup	water	¾ cup

Add all ingredients in the order suggested by your bread machine manual and process on the basic bread cycle according to the manufacturer's directions.

*After measuring out what is needed for this recipe, be sure to replenish your sourdough starter with equal amounts of flour and water.

PER (1-OUNCE) SERVING: 78 Calories; .4 gm. Fat; 0 mg. Cholesterol; 5% Calories from Fat

Kale and Yogurt Bread

If you need extra calcium, this is your bread. For a sandwich, fill with tangy slices of tomato aspic or a slice of tomato and a crumble of feta cheese.

SMALL LOAF (1 POUND)	INGREDIENTS	LARGE LOAF (1½ POUNDS)
½ pound	fresh kale leaves, tough stems removed	¾ pound
1 teaspoon	dry yeast	1½ teaspoons
1¾ cups	bread flour	2⅔ cups
½ cup	whole wheat flour	¾ cup
1 teaspoon	grated nutmeg	1½ teaspoons
1 teaspoon	dried minced onion	1½ teaspoons
½ teaspoon	salt	¾ teaspoon
¼ cup	nonfat plain yogurt	⅓ cup
2	egg whites	3
⅓ cup	water	½ cup

1. Coarsely shred the kale. Cook in a large saucepan of boiling salted water until very tender, 15 to 20 minutes, or longer if the kale is tough; drain. Rinse under cold water until cool enough to handle. Squeeze dry and finely chop the kale. Squeeze again to remove as much moisture as possible. Measure out ½ cup (¾ cup) chopped kale for this recipe. Reserve any remaining for another use.

2. Add all ingredients in the order suggested by your bread machine manual and process on the basic bread cycle according to the manufacturer's directions.

PER (1-OUNCE) SERVING: 74 Calories; .4 gm. Fat; .1 mg. Cholesterol; 5% Calories from Fat

Sweet Potato and Green Apple Bread

This bright sandwich bread packs in the vitamins. Fill slices with assertive vegetables like thinly sliced radishes or radish sprouts, slivered turnips, scallions, or arugula. Spicy chicken or tuna salad go well, too.

SMALL LOAF (1 POUND)	INGREDIENTS	LARGE LOAF (1½ POUNDS)
1 teaspoon	dry yeast	1½ teaspoons
2 cups	bread flour	3 cups
½ cup	yellow cornmeal	¾ cup
½ cup	mashed sweet potato	¾ cup
¼ cup	chopped green apple, (including the peel)	⅓ cup
¼ teaspoon	salt	½ teaspoon
¾ cup	water	1 cup plus 2 tablespoons

Add all ingredients in the order suggested by your bread machine manual and process on the basic bread cycle according to the manufacturer's directions.

PER (1-OUNCE) SERVING: 90 Calories; .4 gm. Fat; 0 mg. Cholesterol; 4% Calories from Fat

Spiced Sweet Potato Bread

This soft, moist bread, with a gentle kick of pepper, makes fine chicken and cucumber sandwiches. For a warm open-faced sandwich, toast, top with sliced banana, fresh pineapple, or well-drained canned pineapple and broil briefly until brown.

SMALL LOAF (1 POUND)	INGREDIENTS	LARGE LOAF (1½ POUNDS)
1 teaspoon	dry yeast	1½ teaspoons
1¾ cups	bread flour	2⅔ cups
½ cup	whole wheat flour	¾ cup
½ cup	mashed sweet potato	¾ cup
¼ teaspoon	ground cloves	½ teaspoon
¼ teaspoon	freshly ground black pepper	½ teaspoon
½ teaspoon	salt	¾ teaspoon
⅔ cup	water	1 cup

Add all ingredients in the order suggested by your bread machine manual and process on the basic bread cycle according to the manufacturer's directions.

PER (1-OUNCE) SERVING: 78 Calories; .4 gm. Fat; 0 mg. Cholesterol; 4% Calories from Fat

Thanksgiving Bread

When we spent Thanksgiving weekend with Aunt Mimi and Uncle George, my cousins and I made turkey sandwiches late Thanksgiving night because during the afternoon feast, there were too many other enticing vegetables and desserts to distract us. Turkey still tastes best to me inside a sandwich with mayonnaise and cranberries, and this is the bread to use.

SMALL LOAF (1 POUND)	INGREDIENTS	LARGE LOAF (1½ POUNDS)
1¼ teaspoons	dry yeast	1¾ teaspoons
2 cups	bread flour	3 cups
¼ cup	wheat bran	⅓ cup
¼ cup	mashed cooked sweet potato	⅓ cup
1 tablespoon	grated orange zest	1½ tablespoons
½ teaspoon	salt	¾ teaspoon
1 tablespoon	apple butter (no sugar added)	1½ tablespoons
⅔ cup	water	¾ cup plus 2 tablespoons
½ cup	fresh cranberries	¾ cup

1. Add all the ingredients except the cranberries in the order suggested by your bread machine manual and process according to the manufacturer's directions.
2. Add the cranberries at the beeper or at the end of the first kneading in machines without a beeper to signal addition of fruit and nuts.

PER (1-OUNCE) SERVING: 75 Calories; .3 gm. Fat; 0 mg. Cholesterol; 4% Calories from Fat

Sprouted Wheat and Orange Bread

To sprout wheat, you must plan ahead. Three days before you want to make the bread, add 2 cups of water to ¼ cup of wheatberries in a one-quart plastic or glass container. Cover with cheesecloth or clean, thin cotton fabric held on with a rubber band and leave the container in a dark place overnight. Drain the water off through the fabric. Add fresh water, swish it around gently, and pour it off again. Repeat this rinsing process twice a day until the berry sprouts are as long as the berries, not longer.

SMALL LOAF (1 POUND)	INGREDIENTS	LARGE LOAF (1½ POUNDS)
1 teaspoon	dry yeast	1½ teaspoons
2 cups	bread flour	3 cups
½ cup	sprouted wheatberries	¾ cup
2 tablespoons	wheat bran	3 tablespoons
2 tablespoons	nonfat dry milk	3 tablespoons
½ teaspoon	ground ginger	¾ teaspoon
2 teaspoons	grated orange zest	1 tablespoon
½ teaspoon	salt	¾ teaspoon
⅔ cup	water	1 cup

Add all ingredients in the order suggested by your bread machine manual and process on the basic bread cycle according to the manufacturer's directions.

PER (1-OUNCE) SERVING: 75 Calories; .4 gm. Fat; .1 mg. Cholesterol; 5% Calories from Fat

Triple Wheat Bread

Slice this high-fiber bread thin and fill with radishes, tomatoes, and sprouts or with turkey breast. To avoid fat, spread the turkey sandwich with salsa instead of mayonnaise.

SMALL LOAF (1 POUND)	INGREDIENTS	LARGE LOAF (1½ POUNDS)
1¼ teaspoons	dry yeast	2 teaspoons
1¾ cups	bread flour	2⅔ cups
½ cup	whole wheat flour	¾ cup
½ cup	cooked wheatberries (see page 5)	¾ cup
2 tablespoons	nonfat dry milk	3 tablespoons
½ teaspoon	salt	¾ teaspoon
½ cup	mashed banana	¾ cup
½ cup	water	¾ cup

Add all ingredients in the order suggested by your bread machine manual and process on the basic bread cycle according to the manufacturer's directions.

PER (1-OUNCE) SERVING: 85 Calories; .4 gm. Fat; .1 mg. Cholesterol; 5% Calories from Fat

Roasted Onion and Orange Whole Wheat Bread

Use subtle fillings for this sandwich bread so that the delicate blend of browned onion, black pepper, orange, and wheat comes through. Try sliced turkey and Bibb lettuce, or a slice of pear with a sprinkle of crumbled blue cheese.

SMALL LOAF (1 POUND)	INGREDIENTS	LARGE LOAF (1½ POUNDS)
1¼ teaspoons	dry yeast	2 teaspoons
1¼ cups	bread flour	2 cups
1 cup	whole wheat flour	1½ cups
2 tablespoons	rolled oats	3 tablespoons
¼ cup	chopped roasted onion*	⅓ cup
2 teaspoons	grated orange zest	1 tablespoon
⅛ teaspoon	freshly ground black pepper	¼ teaspoon
½ teaspoon	salt	¾ teaspoon
½ cup	water	¾ cup

Add all ingredients in the order suggested by your bread machine manual and process on the basic bread cycle according to the manufacturer's directions.

*To roast an onion, preheat the oven to 450 degrees. Place an unpeeled onion on a square of aluminum foil and roast for 45 to 60 minutes, until soft. Peel when cool.

PER (1-OUNCE) SERVING: 69 Calories; .4 gm. Fat; 0 mg. Cholesterol; 5% Calories from Fat

One Hundred Percent Whole Wheat Bread

If your machine has a whole wheat cycle, use it and bake the bread in the machine. If not, make the bread on the dough cycle and follow the second option (Steps 1 to 3).

SMALL LOAF (1 POUND)	INGREDIENTS	LARGE LOAF (1½ POUNDS)
1½ teaspoons	dry yeast	2¼ teaspoons
2½ cups	whole wheat flour	3¾ cups
2 tablespoons	nonfat powdered milk	3 tablespoons
2 teaspoons	vital wheat gluten*	1 tablespoon
2 tablespoons	grated orange zest	3 tablespoons
½ teaspoon	salt	¾ teaspoon
2 tablespoons	minced prunes**	3 tablespoons
¾ cup plus 2 tablespoons	water	1¼ cups

If you have a machine with a whole wheat setting, add all ingredients in the order suggested by your bread machine manual and process on the whole wheat cycle according to the manufacturer's directions.

OR

1. If you do not have a whole wheat setting, add all ingredients for the dough in the order suggested by your bread machine manual and process on the dough cycle according to the manufacturer's directions.

2. At the end of the dough cycle, remove the dough from the machine. Spray a 1-pound loaf pan with vegetable oil. Add dough, cover loosely, and let rise in a draft-free place about 45 minutes.

3. While the dough is rising, preheat the oven to 350 degrees. When the dough has doubled in size, bake 35 to 45 minutes. Turn out of the pan and let cool completely.

*Vital wheat gluten is available at health food stores.
**If the prunes are hard, pour boiling water over them to soften, then drain well.

PER (1-OUNCE) SERVING: 73 Calories; .4 gm. Fat; .1 mg. Cholesterol; 5% Calories from Fat

Whole Wheat Bread with Rosemary

For an unusual sandwich, fill this bread with mashed white beans, snips of sun-dried tomato, and crisp romaine lettuce. Or slip a little leftover roast lamb under the lettuce.

SMALL LOAF (1 POUND)	INGREDIENTS	LARGE LOAF (1½ POUNDS)
1½ teaspoons	dry yeast	2¼ teaspoons
1¼ cups	bread flour	2 cups
1 cup	whole wheat flour	1½ cups
1 tablespoon	vital wheat gluten*	1½ tablespoons
2 teaspoons	dried rosemary	1 tablespoon
½ teaspoon	salt	¾ teaspoon
¼ cup	mashed ripe banana	⅓ cup
¾ cup plus 2 tablespoons	water	1 cup plus 2 tablespoons

Add all ingredients in the order suggested by your bread machine manual and process on the basic bread cycle according to the manufacturer's directions.

*Vital wheat gluten is available at health food stores.

PER (1-OUNCE) SERVING: 71 Calories; .4 gm. Fat; 0 mg. Cholesterol; 4% Calories from Fat

Low-Fat Crusty Whole Wheat Bread

Soft inside and crusty outside, this is a favorite for any meal, and it keeps well. Toast it for breakfast or make it into a tuna or sardine and tomato sandwich for lunch.

SMALL LOAF (1 POUND)	INGREDIENTS	LARGE LOAF (1½ POUNDS)
1½ teaspoons	dry yeast	2¼ teaspoons
1½ cups	bread flour	2¼ cups
¾ cup	whole wheat flour	1 cup plus 2 tablespoons
2 tablespoons	nonfat dry milk	3 tablespoons
1 teaspoon	salt	1½ teaspoons
2 tablespoons	minced prunes*	3 tablespoons
¾ cup plus 2 tablespoons	water	1¼ cups

Add all ingredients in the order suggested by your bread machine manual and process on the basic bread cycle according to the manufacturer's directions.

*If the prunes are hard, pour boiling water over them to soften, then drain well.

PER (1-OUNCE) SERVING: 71 Calories; .3 gm. Fat; .1 mg. Cholesterol; 4% Calories from Fat

Whole Wheat Baguettes

These long, crisp loaves are a nutritious variation on the French classic. Serve with soups, salads, and dishes with rich sauces. Or top a crusty piece with a slice of summer tomato and a sprinkle of fresh basil.

Yield: 2 (15- to 18-inch-long) baguettes   *3 baguettes*
   6 servings per baguette

SMALL LOAF (1 POUND)	INGREDIENTS	LARGE LOAF (1½ POUNDS)
1½ teaspoons	dry yeast	2¼ teaspoons
1½ cups	bread flour	2¼ cups
¾ cup	whole wheat flour	1 cup plus 2 tablespoons
1 teaspoon	salt	1½ teaspoons
¾ cup plus 2 tablespoons	water	1¼ cups
2 teaspoons	sesame seeds	1 tablespoon

1. Add all ingredients for the dough except the sesame seeds in the order suggested by your bread machine manual and process on the dough cycle according to the manufacturer's directions.

2. At the end of the dough cycle, remove the dough from the machine and divide it in half (thirds). On a lightly floured board with barely floured hands, roll each piece into a rope 15 to 18 inches long. The width of your oven and your longest baking sheet will determine the length. Sprinkle sesame seeds on the board. Press one side of each baguette into the seeds. Place the breads sesame seed-side up 4 inches apart on a nonstick baking sheet. Let rise in a draft-free place 20 minutes, or until doubled in size.

3. While the breads are rising, preheat the oven to 400 degrees. When the loaves have doubled in size, slash the tops diagonally in 2 or 3 places with a sharp knife or single-edged razor. Bake 20 minutes, or until golden brown.

PER SERVING: 89 Calories; .5 gm. Fat; 0 mg. Cholesterol; 5% Calories from Fat

Summer Zucchini Bread

Even if you are not a gardener, at the height of summer, zucchini is cheap and plentiful. A loaf of this bread uses more than a cup of zucchini and makes excellent tuna, chicken, or apple salad sandwiches.

SMALL LOAF (1 POUND)	INGREDIENTS	LARGE LOAF (1½ POUNDS)
1 teaspoon	dry yeast	1½ teaspoons
2 cups	bread flour	3 cups
¼ cup	whole wheat flour	⅓ cup
2 teaspoons	dried minced onion	1 tablespoon
¼ teaspoon	garlic powder	½ teaspoon
½ teaspoon	salt	¾ teaspoon
1 cup	grated zucchini	1½ cups
2 tablespoons	minced sun-dried tomatoes*	3 tablespoons
⅓ cup	water	½ cup

Add all ingredients in the order suggested by your bread machine manual and process on the basic bread cycle according to the manufacturer's directions.

*Pour boiling water over the sun-dried tomato halves. Soak 10 minutes, drain, and let cool to room temperature. With a scissors, snip into ¼-inch pieces. Do not use dried tomatoes that are reconstituted and packed in oil for this recipe.

PER (1-OUNCE) SERVING: 73 Calories; .4 gm. Fat; 0 mg. Cholesterol; 4% Calories from Fat

Chapter Three

Hors D'Oeuvres, First-Course Breads, and Snacks

This is the chapter where you really get to be creative. Many of these recipes use dough that is made in the bread machine, then shaped by hand, and baked on the stovetop or in a conventional oven. Dumplings, turnovers, and Indian flat breads are filled with low-fat, sugar-free savories. While the machine makes the dough, you can make the filling, so that the total preparation time is not very long. And many of these hors d'oeuvres can serve equally well as light lunch dishes or as part of a buffet or as first courses at dinner and snacks in between.

Finished loaves in this chapter possess exceptionally striking flavors. They need little or no filling to make you happy nibbling them out of hand. Argue politics while munching Jalapeño Whole Wheat Bread. Make a friend or a date while sharing a Spinach and Potato Dalpuri. Get to know someone better between bites of Provençal Bread. Do business deals over Herbed Bread Sticks, rather than over peanuts and martinis. Celebrate the soccer championship with a Mediterranean Vegetable Pizza or Salsa Bread.

Bread and wine alone can be a party. Can it get any better

than watching the sun set with Sicilian Bread and a bottle of chilled dry white wine? How about hot mulled cider with Herbed Potato Turnovers by the fireside after skating or skiing?

If you keep Focaccia or sliced Garlic and Greens Bread in the freezer, either can become an instant first course or hors d'oeuvre for unexpected guests—the host whips up the main course while the guests nibble and talk. Put your bread machine in the cupboard; the party is underway.

Amaranth Bread with Sun-Dried Tomatoes

Slice the bread, toast, and rub with garlic. Cover the slice with salad greens for an open-faced sandwich in summer or cut into quarters for an easy, light hors d'oeuvre. Save the last piece to make croutons for soup or salad.

SMALL LOAF (1 POUND)	INGREDIENTS	LARGE LOAF (1½ POUNDS)
¼ cup	boiling water	⅓ cup
¼ cup	amaranth grain	⅓ cup
¼ cup	chopped sun-dried tomatoes*	⅓ cup
1¼ teaspoon	dry yeast	1¾ teaspoons
1⅔ cups	bread flour	2½ cups
½ cup	whole wheat flour	¾ cup
2 tablespoons	nonfat dry milk	3 tablespoons
¾ teaspoon	salt	1 teaspoon
⅔ cup	water	1 cup

1. Pour the ¼ (⅓ cup) cup boiling water over the amaranth. Return to a boil, remove from the heat, and let cool to room temperature. Drain.

2. Add all ingredients in the order suggested by your bread machine manual and process on the basic bread cycle according to the manufacturer's directions.

*Pour boiling water over sun-dried tomato halves. Soak 10 minutes, drain, and cool to room temperature. With a scissors, snip into ¼-inch pieces. Do not use tomatoes that are reconstituted and packed in oil for this recipe.

PER (1-OUNCE) SERVING: 82 Calories; .5 gm. Fat; .1 mg. Cholesterol; 6% Calories from Fat

Artichoke and Dried Mushroom Bread

SMALL LOAF (1 POUND)	INGREDIENTS	LARGE LOAF (1½ POUNDS)
2 cups	boiling water	2 cups
2 tablespoons	imported dried mushroom pieces	3 tablespoons
1 teaspoon	dry yeast	1½ teaspoons
1½ cups	bread flour	2¼ cups
¾ cup	whole wheat flour	1 cup plus 2 tablespoons
¼ teaspoon	garlic powder	½ teaspoon
1 teaspoon	dried thyme leaves	1½ teaspoons
½ teaspoon	salt	¾ teaspoon
½ cup	diced (½-inch) artichoke hearts	¾ cup

1. Pour boiling water over the mushrooms. Soak ½ hour. Drain the mushrooms, reserving ⅔ cup (1 cup) of the soaking liquid. Coarsely chop the mushrooms.
2. Add all ingredients except the mushrooms and artichokes [but including the reserved ⅔ cup (1 cup) mushroom water] according to your bread machine manual and process on the basic bread cycle according to the manufacturer's directions.
3. Add the artichokes and mushrooms at the beeper or at the end of the first kneading in machines without a beeper to signal addition of fruit and nuts.

PER (1-OUNCE) SERVING: 69 Calories; .3 gm. Fat; 0 mg. Cholesterol; 4% Calories from Fat

Banana Chutney Bread

For an hors d'oeuvre, serve this light but spicy bread with grated cucumber and yogurt salad. Or trim the crusts, slice thin, and toast to accompany curried dishes.

SMALL LOAF (1 POUND)	INGREDIENTS	LARGE LOAF (1½ POUNDS)
1¼ teaspoons	dry yeast	2¼ teaspoons
1½ cups	bread flour	2¼ cups
¾ cup	whole wheat flour	1 cup plus 2 tablespoons
2 tablespoons	nonfat dry milk	3 tablespoons
1 teaspoon	curry powder	1½ teaspoons
1 teaspoon	minced fresh ginger	1½ teaspoons
½ teaspoon	salt	¾ teaspoon
¼ teaspoon	freshly ground black pepper	½ teaspoon
¼ cup	mashed banana	⅓ cup
1 tablespoon	white wine vinegar	1½ tablespoons
¾ cup plus 2 tablespoons	water	1¼ cups
¼ cup	raisins	⅓ cup

1. Add all ingredients except the raisins according to your bread machine manual and process on the basic bread cycle according to the manufacturer's directions.
2. Add the raisins at the beeper or at the end of the first kneading in machines without a beeper to signal addition of fruit and nuts.

PER (1-OUNCE) SERVING: 79 Calories; .4 gm. Fat; .1 mg. Cholesterol; 4% Calories from Fat

Riviera Bread

SMALL LOAF (1 POUND)	INGREDIENTS	LARGE LOAF (1½ POUNDS)
⅓ cup	boiling water	½ cup
¼ teaspoon	saffron threads	¼ teaspoon
1½ teaspoons	dry yeast	2¼ teaspoons
1¾ cups	bread flour	2⅔ cups
½ cup	whole wheat flour	¾ cup
1	garlic clove(s), minced	1½
½ teaspoon	fennel seeds or aniseed	¾ teaspoon
1 teaspoon	dried thyme leaves	1½ teaspoons
¼ teaspoon	freshly ground black pepper	½ teaspoon
1 tablespoon	grated orange zest	1½ tablespoons
1 teaspoon	dried minced onion	1½ teaspoons
¼ cup	chopped sun-dried tomatoes*	⅓ cup
½ teaspoon	salt	¾ teaspoon
½ cup	clam juice	¾ cup

1. Pour boiling water over the saffron. Let cool.

2. Add all ingredients in the order suggested by your bread machine manual and process on the basic bread cycle according to the manufacturer's directions.

*Pour boiling water over the sun-dried tomato halves. Soak for 10 minutes, drain, and cool to room temperature. With a scissors, snip into ¼-inch pieces. Do not use tomatoes that are reconstituted and packed in oil for this recipe.

PER (1-OUNCE) SERVING: 73 Calories; .4 gm. Fat; 0 mg. Cholesterol; 4% Calories from Fat

Herbed Bread Sticks

These crisp, earthy treats look as good as they taste. Stand them up in a pitcher or mug and make them the centerpiece of your dinner table, for as long as they last.

Yield: 36 bread sticks

1¼ teaspoons	dry yeast
1½ cups	bread flour
¾ cup	whole wheat flour
1 tablespoon	dried rosemary or thyme leaves
¼ cup	minced prunes*
¾ teaspoon	salt
¾ cup plus 2 tablespoons	water

1. Add all ingredients for the dough in the order suggested by your bread machine manual and process on the dough cycle according to the manufacturer's directions.
2. When the dough cycle ends, remove the dough from the machine. Preheat the oven to 400 degrees. Cut the dough into pieces as big as a walnut. On a floured board, roll each ball into a rope about ½ inch thick. Place 1 inch apart on a nonstick baking sheet and bake right away 10 to 15 minutes, or until golden.

*If the prunes are hard, pour boiling water over them to soften, then drain well.

PER BREAD STICK: 32 Calories; .1 gm. Fat; 0 mg. Cholesterol; 4% Calories from Fat

Bread Basket

The fanciest thing I saw at Lutèce, one of New York's fanciest restaurants, was a basket made of bread and filled with baby greens. The waiter informed me that this was the garnish for the pâté of thrush. Without the thrush, this is an elegant presentation. Use the basket as salad bowls—with vegetable, seafood, or chicken salad. When they have absorbed the salad dressing, they will taste marvelous. Fill the baskets just before serving.

Yield: 6 baskets

---

1 teaspoon	dry yeast
1¾ cups	bread flour
½ cup	whole wheat flour
½ teaspoon	salt
¾ cup plus 1 tablespoon	water
1	egg white

1. Add all ingredients except egg white in the order suggested by your bread machine manual and process on the dough cycle according to the manufacturer's directions.

2. At the end of the dough cycle, remove the bread from the machine. Preheat the oven to 400 degrees. Grease the outside of 6 large (2-cup) custard cups or ovenproof bowls. Turn the bowls upside down on a nonstick baking sheet(s), leaving 4 inches between bowls.

3. Cut the dough into 6 pieces. On a floured board, gently roll each piece into a 30-inch-long rope. Starting at the bottom of a bowl, wind the rope around and around loosely, covering the bowl and ending in a coil on the top. Do not worry about open spaces since the dough will rise and come together. Repeat with the other 5 bowls and pieces of dough. Brush with egg white, being careful not to get any on the bowl. Let rise in a draft-free place for ½ hour.

4. Bake 15 minutes. Remove from the oven. Turn each basket upside-down, remove the bowls (with a potholder), and return the bread baskets to the oven another 10 to 15 minutes, until brown. If not using the same day, carefully wrap in freezer paper or plastic and freeze.

PER (1-OUNCE) SERVING: 186 Calories; 1.4 gm. Fat; 0 mg. Cholesterol, 7% Calories from Fat

Chestnut Bread

SMALL LOAF (1 POUND)	INGREDIENTS	LARGE LOAF (1½ POUNDS)
½ pound	chestnuts	¾ pound
1¼ teaspoons	dry yeast	2 teaspoons
¾ cup	water	1 cup plus 2 tablespoons
½ cup	whole wheat flour	¾ cup
2 cups	bread flour	3 cups
½ teaspoon	salt	¾ teaspoon
¼ cup	minced prunes*	⅓ cup

1. Preheat the oven to 350 degrees. Cut a cross in the top of each chestnut. Bake 30 minutes, cool, and peel. Chop coarsely. You should have at least ½ (¾) cup of chestnuts.

2. Mix the yeast, water, whole wheat flour, and ½ cup (¾ cup) of the bread flour. Stir into a thick paste, cover, and let rise in a draft-free place an hour. This is the "sponge."

3. Add the sponge, the remaining 1½ (2¼) cups bread flour, the salt, minced prunes, and the chestnuts in the order suggested by your bread machine manual, including the sponge with the liquid ingredients, and process on the basic bread cycle according to the manufacturer's directions.

*If the prunes are hard, pour boiling water over them to soften, then drain well.

PER (1-OUNCE) SERVING: 123 Calories; .8 gm. Fat; 0 mg. Cholesterol; 6% Calories from Fat

Spicy Chickpea Bread

In Trinidad, similar ingredients are made into a batter, deep-fried, and doused with hot pepper sauce. This bread captures the flavor without the oil. Filled with salad, it tastes like falafel.

SMALL LOAF (1 POUND)	INGREDIENTS	LARGE LOAF (1½ POUNDS)
⅓ cup	canned chickpeas, drained	½ cup
1	garlic clove(s)	1½
⅔ cup plus 3 tablespoons	water	1¼ cups
1½ teaspoons	dry yeast	2¼ teaspoons
1¾ cups	bread flour	2⅔ cups
¼ cup	whole wheat flour	⅓ cup
1 teaspoon	grated lemon zest	1½ teaspoons
½ teaspoon	ground cumin	¾ teaspoon
¼ teaspoon	ground coriander	½ teaspoon
⅛ teaspoon	cayenne	¼ teaspoon
½ teaspoon	salt	¾ teaspoon

1. In a blender or food processor, puree the chickpeas with the garlic and 3 tablespoons (¼ cup) of the water.
2. Add all ingredients including the chickpea puree in the order suggested by your bread machine manual and process on the basic bread cycle according to the manufacturer's directions.

PER (1-OUNCE) SERVING: 66 Calories; .4 gm. Fat; 0 mg. Cholesterol; 5% Calories from Fat

Double Corn Bread

SMALL LOAF (1 POUND)	INGREDIENTS	LARGE LOAF (1½ POUNDS)
1¼ teaspoons	dry yeast	2 teaspoons
1¾ cups	bread flour	2⅔ cups
¾ cup	yellow cornmeal	1 cup plus 2 tablespoons
1 teaspoon	ground cumin	1½ teaspoons
2 teaspoons	vital wheat gluten*	1 tablespoon
¾ teaspoon	salt	1 teaspoon
2 tablespoons	minced prunes**	3 tablespoons
¾ cup plus 2 tablespoons	water	1¼ cups
¼ cup	corn kernels	⅓ cup

1. Add all ingredients except the corn kernels in the order suggested by your bread machine manual and process on the basic bread cycle according to the manufacturer's directions.

2. Add the corn at the beeper or at the end of the first kneading in machines without a beeper to signal addition of fruit and nuts.

*Vital wheat gluten is available at health food stores.
**If the prunes are hard, pour boiling water over them to soften, then drain well.

PER (1-OUNCE) SERVING: 86 Calories; .4 gm. Fat; 0 mg. Cholesterol; 4% Calories from Fat

Dilled Cucumber and Yogurt Bread

Smoked fish, especially salmon, covering this bread makes a delicate hors d'oeuvre or open-faced sandwich. Or slice the bread thick, toast, and spread with yogurt cheese jazzed up with horseradish or grated ginger.

SMALL LOAF (1 POUND)	INGREDIENTS	LARGE LOAF (1½ POUNDS)
1 teaspoon	dry yeast	1½ teaspoons
1¾ cups	bread flour	2⅔ cups
½ cup	whole wheat flour	¾ cup
2 tablespoons	nonfat dry milk	3 tablespoons
½ cup	peeled and minced cucumber	¾ cup
2 tablespoons	mashed banana	3 tablespoons
2 tablespoons	dried dill weed	3 tablespoons
½ teaspoon	salt	¾ teaspoon
Pinch	baking soda	⅛ teaspoon
⅓ cup	nonfat plain yogurt	½ cup
⅓ cup	water	½ cup

Add all ingredients in the order suggested by your bread machine manual and process on the basic bread cycle according to the manufacturer's directions.

PER (1-OUNCE) SERVING: 75 Calories; .3 gm. Fat; .2 mg. Cholesterol; 4% Calories from Fat

Caramelized Cabbage Dalpuri

Cut this filled flat bread into wedges for a savory first course or hors d'oeuvre.

Yield: 4 (7-inch) flat breads, 8 servings

FILLING

---

3 cups	finely shredded cabbage
1	garlic clove, minced
¼ cup	frozen apple juice concentrate, thawed
1 tablespoon	balsamic vinegar
⅛ teaspoon	freshly ground black pepper

DOUGH

1½ teaspoons	dry yeast
1¾ cups	bread flour
¼ cup	rye flour
1 teaspoon	caraway seeds
½ teaspoon	salt
¼ cup	sourdough starter*
⅔ cup	water

1. In a large nonstick skillet, cook the cabbage, garlic, and apple juice over low heat ½ hour, stirring occasionally. Add the vinegar and pepper, cover, and cook 5 to 10 minutes longer, until the liquids are absorbed. Cool.

2. Add all ingredients for the dough in the order suggested by your bread machine manual and process on the dough cycle according to the manufacturer's directions.

---

3. At the end of the dough cycle, remove the dough from the machine, and divide into 4 equal parts. With floured hands, roll each piece of dough into a ball. With your thumb, make a large indentation in each piece. Add 2 tablespoons of filling and pull the dough up around the filling, pinching the ends together securely to seal.

4. Place a piece of plastic wrap or wax paper on top of each ball of dough. Then press down with the bottom of a heavy skillet to flatten each into a round less than ½ inch thick.

5. In a nonstick skillet, cook the *dalpuri* over medium heat 10 minutes on each side, or until golden brown and cooked through. Cut into wedges and eat warm.

*After measuring out what is needed for this recipe, be sure to replenish your sourdough starter with equal amounts of flour and water.

PER SERVING: 155 Calories; 1.2 gm. Fat; 0 mg. Cholesterol; 7% Calories from Fat

---

Corn and Black Bean Dalpuri

This is an East Indian-style bread with a Tex-Mex taste. Serve as a spicy first course with a plain yogurt sauce.

Yield: 4 (7-inch) flat breads, 8 servings

FILLING

½ cup	black beans, cooked or canned
½	minced fresh jalapeño pepper or ¼ teaspoon crushed hot pepper
1 teaspoon	ground cumin
½ teaspoon	ground coriander
¼ teaspoon	garlic powder

DOUGH

1¼ teaspoons	dry yeast
1¾ cups	bread flour
½ cup	yellow cornmeal
1 teaspoon	ground chili powder
½ teaspoon	salt
1	egg white
⅔ cup	water

1. Mash the beans and mix with all other ingredients for the filling.
2. Add all ingredients for the dough in the order suggested by your bread machine manual and process on the dough cycle according to the manufacturer's directions.

3. At the end of the dough cycle, remove the dough from the machine and divide into 4 equal parts. With floured hands, roll each piece of dough into a ball. With your thumb, make a large indentation in each piece. Add 2 tablespoons of filling and pull the dough up around the filling, pinching the ends together securely to seal.

4. Place a piece of plastic wrap or wax paper on top of each ball of dough. Then press down with the bottom of a heavy skillet to flatten each into a round less than ½ inch thick. Repeat with remaining dough and filling.

5. In a nonstick skillet, cook the *dalpuri* over medium heat 10 minutes on each side, or until golden brown. Cut into wedges and eat warm.

PER SERVING: 164 Calories; 1.3 gm. Fat; 0 mg. Cholesterol; 7% Calories from Fat

Spinach and Potato Dalpuri

Dalpuri, *a crusty flat bread with a surprise filling, was popularized in the Caribbean by emigrés from India. Slice it into wedges for an hors d'oeuvre or serve whole for an entrée.*

Yield: 4 (7-inch) flat breads, 8 servings

FILLING

1 (10-ounce) package	frozen chopped spinach, thawed
½ cup	mashed potato
½ teaspoon	dried rosemary
¼ teaspoon	garlic powder
¼ teaspoon	salt
⅛ teaspoon	freshly ground black pepper

DOUGH

1½ teaspoons	dry yeast
1¾ cups	bread flour
½ cup	whole wheat flour
½ teaspoon	salt
2 tablespoons	minced prunes*
¾ cup	water

1. In a kitchen towel or piece of clean, thin fabric, squeeze the water out of the spinach. Measure out ½ cup of spinach; reserve the rest for another use. Mix the spinach with all the other ingredients for the filling.

---

2. Add all ingredients for the dough in the order suggested by your bread machine manual and process on the dough cycle according to the manufacturer's directions.
3. At the end of the dough cycle, remove the dough from the machine and divide into 4 equal parts. With floured hands roll each piece of dough into a ball. With your thumb, make a large indentation in each piece. Add 3 tablespoons of filling and pull the dough up around the filling, pinching the ends together securely to seal.
4. Place a piece of plastic wrap or wax paper on top of each ball of dough. Then press down with the bottom of a heavy skillet to flatten each into a round less than ½ inch thick.
5. In a nonstick pan, cook the *dalpuri* over medium heat 10 minutes on each side, or until golden brown. Cut into wedges and eat warm.

*If the prunes are hard, pour boiling water over them to soften, then drain well.

PER SERVING: 156 Calories; .1 gm. Fat; 0 mg. Cholesterol; 5% Calories from Fat

---

Chinese Wild Mushroom Dumplings

Serve these baked dim sum with rice wine vinegar or light soy sauce for dipping. The number of servings here depends upon whether you are offering the dumplings as an hors d'oeuvre, snack, or light vegetarian lunch. Nutritional counts below are given per dumpling.

Yield: 24 dumplings

DOUGH

2 teaspoons	dry yeast
1¾ cups	bread flour
½ cup	whole wheat flour
½ teaspoon	salt
¾ cup	water

FILLING

12	shiitake mushrooms, coarsely chopped, or sliced cremini mushrooms
2	garlic cloves, minced
24	cilantro leaves

1. Add all ingredients for the dough in the order suggested by your bread machine manual and process on the dough cycle according to the manufacturer's directions.
2. When the dough cycle ends, remove the dough from the machine and divide in half. Roll each piece between your palms into a 12-inch rope. Cut each rope into 12 equal (1-inch) parts. Roll or pull each piece into a 3-inch round.

---

3. Spoon a few pieces of mushroom, garlic, and a cilantro leaf in the center of each round. Pull the edges of the dough up and pinch together firmly to enclose the filling and seal. Place the dumplings pinched sides-down 1 inch apart on a nonstick baking sheet. Cover lightly and let rise in a draft-free place 30 minutes, or until doubled in size.

4. Meanwhile, preheat the oven to 375 degrees. When the dough has doubled in size, bake the dumplings 15 minutes, or until golden.

PER DUMPLING: 48 Calories; .2 gm. Fat; 0 mg. Cholesterol; 4% Calories from Fat

Spiced Fig Bread

Here is a high-fiber, fruity bread with the pleasing, delicate crunch of fig seeds. Cinnamon, nutmeg, and cloves add enough spicy interest to make slices tasty to eat plain.

SMALL LOAF (1 POUND)	INGREDIENTS	LARGE LOAF (1½ POUNDS)
1 teaspoon	dry yeast	1½ teaspoons
2 cups	bread flour	3 cups
¼ cup	wheat bran	⅓ cup
2 tablespoons	rolled oats	3 tablespoons
2 tablespoons	nonfat dry milk	3 tablespoons
1 teaspoon	ground cinnamon	1½ teaspoons
½ teaspoon	ground nutmeg	¾ teaspoon
¼ teaspoon	ground cloves	½ teaspoon
½ teaspoon	salt	¾ teaspoon
½ cup	minced figs*	¾ cup
¾ cup	water	1 cup plus 2 tablespoons

Add all ingredients in the order suggested by your bread machine manual and process on the basic bread cycle according to the manufacturer's directions.

*If the figs are hard, pour boiling water over them to soften, then drain well.

PER (1-OUNCE) SERVING: 88 Calories; .5 gm. Fat; .1 mg. Cholesterol; 5% Calories from Fat

Rosemary and Thyme Fougasse

Fougasse *is a leaf-shaped flat bread that can begin as a table decoration and end in pieces torn off to eat with dinner. It is a pretty, perfumed gift.*

Yield: 2 flat breads, 6 servings each

1 teaspoon	dry yeast
1½ cups	bread flour
¾ cup	whole wheat flour
1 teaspoon	dried thyme leaves
1 teaspoon	dried rosemary
½ teaspoon	salt
¼ cup	nonfat plain yogurt
¾ cup	water

1. Add all ingredients in the order suggested by your bread machine manual and process on the dough cycle according to the manufacturer's directions.

2. At the end of the dough cycle, remove the dough from the machine and divide in half. Preheat the oven to 375 degrees. On a floured board with floured hands, press each piece into a leaf shape about 12 inches long and 8 inches across. Pinch one end to look like a stem. With a sharp knife, cut a slit from an inch above the "stem" to an inch from the top of the leaf. Make other markings with the knife to make the dough look more leaflike.

3. Place the leaves of dough on a nonstick baking sheet(s). Lightly cover and let rise in a draft-free place 15 minutes. Bake 15 minutes, or until golden.

PER SERVING: 92 Calories; .4 gm. Fat; .1 mg. Cholesterol; 4% Calories from Fat

Focaccia

Focaccia is a flat, savory Italian bread. Serve it as a meal preceded by a salad or cut it into small pieces for an hors d'oeuvre.

Yield: 2 (10-inch) focaccias, 4 servings each

DOUGH

---

2 teaspoons	dry yeast
1¾ cups	bread flour
½ cup	whole wheat flour
2 teaspoons	dried rosemary
1 teaspoon	salt
¾ cup plus 2 tablespoons	water

TOPPING

	Vegetable cooking spray
2 cups	thinly sliced onions
1 teaspoon	dried rosemary

1. Add all ingredients for the dough in the order suggested by your bread machine manual and process on the dough cycle according to the manufacturer's directions.
2. While the machine is processing the dough, lightly spray a nonstick skillet with vegetable cooking spray. Add the onions and cook over medium heat, stirring occasionally, 10 minutes, until softened. Cover, reduce the heat to low, and cook 10 minutes longer, until the onions are soft and golden.
3. At the end of the dough cycle, remove the dough from the machine and divide

---

it in half. On a floured board with a floured rolling pin, roll each piece into a 10-inch circle. Place on a nonstick baking sheet(s), cover each with half the onions and half of the rosemary, and let rise in a draft-free place ½ hour.

4. While the dough is rising, preheat the oven to 400 degrees. Bake 15 minutes, or until the crust is golden.

PER SERVING: 154 Calories; .9 gm. Fat; 0 mg. Cholesterol; 5% Calories from Fat

Friselle

My friend Geraldine buys these hard, peppery rolls on Arthur Avenue, the Italian market street in The Bronx. I love to put one in the bottom of a soup bowl and pour chowder over it. When you get to the bottom, the friselle is soft and has absorbed all the goodness of the soup. Or munch on friselle with a glass of red wine.

SMALL LOAF (1 POUND)	INGREDIENTS	LARGE LOAF (1½ POUNDS)
1 teaspoon	dry yeast	1½ teaspoons
1¾ cups	bread flour	2⅔ cups
½ cup	whole wheat flour	¾ cup
½ teaspoon	freshly ground black pepper	¾ teaspoon
½ teaspoon	salt	¾ teaspoon
¾ cup plus 2 tablespoons	water	1¼ cups

1. Add all ingredients in the order suggested by your bread machine manual and process on the basic bread cycle according to the manufacturer's directions.

2. When the bread has cooled, cut the loaf into slices ½ inch thick. Slice each piece into 1-inch fingers. Set on a nonstick baking sheet.

3. Preheat the oven to 300 degrees. Bake the friselle 1 hour, or until golden and hard.

PER (1-OUNCE) SERVING: 68 Calories; .3 gm. Fat; 0 mg. Cholesterol; 4% Calories from Fat

Summer Tomato Galette

Yield: 2 (10-inch) galettes, 6 servings each

8	plum tomatoes
1¼ teaspoons	dry yeast
1½ cups	bread flour
¾ cup	whole wheat flour
1	garlic clove, minced
½ teaspoon	salt
⅛ teaspoon	freshly ground black pepper
¼ cup	mashed banana
¾ cup	water
2 tablespoons	shredded fresh basil

1. Slice the tomatoes ¼ inch thick. Drain on paper towels.

2. Add all ingredients except the tomatoes and basil in the order suggested by your bread machine manual and process on the dough cycle according to the manufacturer's directions.

3. Preheat the oven to 450 degrees. At the end of the dough cycle, remove the dough from the machine. Divide in half. On a floured board with a floured rolling pin, roll each piece into a 10-inch circle. Place dough on a nonstick baking sheet(s). Arrange tomato slices on top in overlapping circles.

4. Bake 20 to 25 minutes, until the crust is brown and tomatoes slightly charred. Sprinkle the basil on top.

PER SERVING: 117 Calories; .8 gm. Fat; 0 mg. Cholesterol; 6% Calories from Fat

Garlic and Greens Bread

SMALL LOAF (1 POUND)	INGREDIENTS	LARGE LOAF (1½ POUNDS)
1 (10-ounce) package	frozen chopped collard or mustard greens or spinach, thawed	1 (10-ounce) package
1 teaspoon	dry yeast	1½ teaspoons
2 cups	bread flour	3 cups
¼ cup	wheat bran	⅓ cup
2 tablespoons	nonfat dry milk	3 tablespoons
1	garlic clove(s), minced	1½
½ teaspoon	salt	¾ teaspoon
2 tablespoons	minced prunes*	3 tablespoons
⅔ cup	water	1 cup

1. In a kitchen towel or clean, thin fabric, squeeze the water out of the greens or spinach. Measure out ½ cup greens (¾ cup for the larger machine) for this recipe. Reserve the rest for another use.

2. Add all ingredients in the order suggested by your bread machine manual and process on the basic bread cycle according to the manufacturer's directions.

*If the prunes are hard, pour boiling water over them to soften, then drain well.

PER (1-OUNCE) SERVING: 72 Calories; .3 gm. Fat; .1 mg. Cholesterol; 4% Calories from Fat

Garlic Knots

Garlic knots are irresistible. Serve along with salad and Italian food or fill with salami and cheese. Try them as sandwiches with tomato and lettuce.

Yield: 12 rolls

1 teaspoon	dry yeast
2 cups	bread flour
1 tablespoon	wheat bran
½ cup	mashed potato
½ teaspoon	salt
½ cup	water
1	garlic clove, minced

1. Add all ingredients except the garlic in the order suggested by your bread machine manual and process on the dough cycle according to the manufacturer's directions.

2. At the end of the dough cycle, remove the dough from the machine and cut into 12 equal pieces. With floured hands, roll each piece into an 8-inch rope. Tie each rope into a loose knot.

3. Preheat the oven to 400 degrees. Dip each knot into the minced garlic and place garlic sides-up on a nonstick baking sheet, cover loosely, and let rise 15 minutes in a draft-free place.

4. Bake 10 to 15 minutes, or until pale gold.

PER ROLL: 91 Calories; .4 gm. Fat; 0 mg. Cholesterol; 3% Calories from Fat

Lebanese Spiced Flat Bread

Zataar (or zatar), a Middle Eastern spice mixture, covers this crisp bread with enough zesty flavor to make it a fine hors d'oeuvre all by itself. No dip or spread is needed.

Yield: 2 (9-by-12-inch) flat breads, 8 servings each

ZATAAR TOPPING

2	medium onions
2 teaspoons	dried thyme leaves
2 teaspoons	dried oregano
½ teaspoon	freshly ground black pepper

DOUGH

1½ teaspoons	dry yeast
1¾ cups	bread flour
½ cup	whole wheat flour
½ teaspoon	salt
¾ cup	water

1. Preheat the oven to 450 degrees. Roast the onions in their skins 45 minutes. Cool and chop into ¼-inch dice. Mix the onions with the thyme, oregano, and pepper to make *zataar*. Leave the oven on.

2. While the onion is roasting, add all ingredients for the dough in the order suggested by your bread machine manual and process on the dough cycle according to the manufacturer's directions.

3. At the end of the dough cycle, remove the dough from the machine and divide in half. On a floured board with a floured rolling pin, roll each piece of dough into a 9-by-12-inch rectangle. Place each on a nonstick baking sheet and spread ½ of the *zataar* mixture over each.

4. Bake immediately 15 to 20 minutes, or until brown on the bottom as well as the top. Serve whole. Each person breaks off a piece to eat with his or her hands.

PER SERVING: 77 Calories; .4 gm. Fat; 0 mg. Cholesterol; 4% Calories from Fat

Leek Pie

A whole meal can grow around this savory pie. Serve it with tomato and tabbouleh salad or potato and sliced beef salad. Or use it as part of a buffet.

Yield: 2 (10-inch) pies, 4 servings each

DOUGH

1¼ teaspoons	dry yeast
1¾ cups	bread flour
½ cup	whole wheat flour
½ teaspoon	salt
½ cup	mashed potato
⅔ cup	water

FILLING

1	large onion
4	large leeks
1 teaspoon	chopped fresh thyme or parsley
⅛ teaspoon	freshly ground black pepper

1. Add all ingredients for the dough in the order suggested by your bread machine manual and process on the dough cycle according to the manufacturer's directions.
2. Preheat the oven to 450 degrees. Place the onion in its skin on a nonstick baking sheet. Bake 40 minutes.
3. Meanwhile, split the leeks lengthwise and rinse well under cold running water. Cut into ½-inch pieces. Cook in a large saucepan of boiling water 10 minutes.

Drain and let cool. When the onion is cool enough to handle, peel it and cut it into ½-inch dice. Reduce the oven temperature to 400 degrees.

4. At the end of the dough cycle, remove the dough from the machine and divide in half. On a floured board with a floured rolling pin, roll each piece into a 12-inch circle. Fit each piece of dough into a 10-inch pie pan, letting the edges overhang the side. Spread ½ of the onions and leeks in each pie, cover, and let rest 15 minutes. Bake 25 minutes, or until the crust is golden brown. Sprinkle with the thyme or parsley and pepper and serve warm.

PER SERVING: 207 Calories; 1 gm. Fat; 0 mg. Cholesterol; 4% Calories from Fat

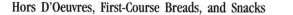

Hot Pepper High-Protein Bread

This sweet, spicy bread can be served in place of a chutney with curried meats, vegetables, or soups. Fill with sliced cucumbers or yogurt cheese for thin sandwiches or serve plain for tea.

SMALL LOAF (1 POUND)	INGREDIENTS	LARGE LOAF (1½ POUNDS)
1¼ teaspoons	dry yeast	2 teaspoons
2 cups	bread flour	3 cups
½ cup	soy flour	¾ cup
2 tablespoons	nonfat dry milk	3 tablespoons
2 tablespoons	wheat bran	3 tablespoons
1 tablespoon	minced fresh jalapeño pepper or ½ teaspoon crushed hot pepper	1½ tablespoons
½ teaspoon	salt	¾ teaspoon
⅓ cup	nonfat plain yogurt	½ cup
2 tablespoons	minced dried figs*	3 tablespoons
¾ cup	water	1 cup plus 2 tablespoons

Add all ingredients in the order suggested by your bread machine manual and process on the basic bread cycle according to the manufacturer's directions.

*If the figs are hard, pour boiling water over them to soften, then drain well.

PER (1-OUNCE) SERVING: 83 Calories; .3 gm. Fat; .2 mg. Cholesterol; 4% Calories from Fat

Moroccan Spiced Bread

Coriander, cinnamon, and cumin are the perfumed Moroccan spices that permeate this tasty bread. Serve as an hors d'oeuvre.

SMALL LOAF (1 POUND)	INGREDIENTS	LARGE LOAF (1½ POUNDS)
1 teaspoon	dry yeast	1½ teaspoons
1½ cups	bread flour	2¼ cups
¾ cup	whole wheat flour	1 cup plus 2 tablespoons
2 tablespoons	minced prunes*	3 tablespoons
1 tablespoon	ground coriander	1½ tablespoons
1 teaspoon	ground ginger	1½ teaspoons
1 teaspoon	ground cumin	1½ teaspoons
1 teaspoon	ground cinnamon	1½ teaspoons
¼ teaspoon	ground turmeric	½ teaspoon
⅛ teaspoon	ground cayenne	¼ teaspoon
2 teaspoons	grated lemon zest	1 tablespoon
½ teaspoon	salt	¾ teaspoon
¾ cup	water	1 cup plus 2 tablespoons

Add all ingredients in the order suggested by your bread machine manual and process on the basic bread cycle according to the manufacturer's directions.

*If the prunes are hard, pour boiling water over them to soften, then drain well.

PER (1-OUNCE) SERVING: 71 Calories; .3 gm. Fat; 0 mg. Cholesterol; 4% Calories from Fat

Pineapple, Bran, and Oat Bread

This bread makes a great afternoon pick-me-up with hot or iced tea. It contributes fiber, vitamin C, and a little protein too.

SMALL LOAF (1 POUND)	INGREDIENTS	LARGE LOAF (1½ POUNDS)
1¼ teaspoons	dry yeast	2 teaspoons
1¾ cups	bread flour	2⅔ cups
¼ cup	rolled oats	⅓ cup
2 tablespoons	wheat bran	3 tablespoons
2 tablespoons	nonfat dry milk	3 tablespoons
1 tablespoon	minced prunes*	1½ tablespoons
¼ teaspoon	ground cloves	¼ teaspoon
1 teaspoon	ground cinnamon	1½ teaspoons
½ teaspoon	salt	¾ teaspoon
½ cup	cubed fresh or drained canned unsweetened pineapple chunks	¾ cup
⅓ cup	water	½ cup

Add all ingredients in the order suggested by your bread machine manual and process on the basic bread cycle according to the manufacturer's directions.

*If the prunes are hard, pour boiling water over them to soften, then drain well.

PER (1-OUNCE) SERVING: 67 Calories; .4 gm. Fat; .1 mg. Cholesterol; 5% Calories from Fat

Polenta Bread with Rosemary and Garlic

Slice thin and cut into triangles. Toast lightly and serve alone or with Italian-style salsa made with tomato, hot pepper, and olives. Or top with grilled chicken or grilled vegetables for an open-faced sandwich.

SMALL LOAF (1 POUND)	INGREDIENTS	LARGE LOAF (1½ POUNDS)
1 teaspoon	dry yeast	1½ teaspoons
2 cups	bread flour	3 cups
¼ cup	yellow cornmeal	⅓ cup
1 teaspoon	dried rosemary	1½ teaspoons
1	garlic clove(s), chopped	1½
½ teaspoon	salt	¾ teaspoon
¾ cup plus 2 tablespoons	water	1¼ cups

Add all ingredients in the order suggested by your bread machine manual and process on the basic bread cycle according to the manufacturer's directions.

PER (1-OUNCE) SERVING: 66 Calories; .4 gm. Fat; 0 mg. Cholesterol; 5% Calories from Fat

Fresh Tomato Pizza

If you leave off the topping, this recipe makes a great herbed foccacia. Bake one crust and freeze one (two) to use later or have a party. Each 10-inch pizza will serve 4 people.

Yield: 2 (10-inch) pizzas, 8 servings; 3 (10-inch) pizzas, 12 servings

DOUGH		
1½ teaspoons	dry yeast	2¼ teaspoons
1½ cups	bread flour	2¼ cups
¾ cup	whole wheat flour	1 cup plus 2 tablespoons
½ cup	mashed potato	¾ cup
1 teaspoon	dried oregano	1½ teaspoons
1 teaspoon	dried thyme leaves	1½ teaspoons
½ teaspoon	salt	¾ teaspoon
¾ cup	water	1 cup plus 2 tablespoons

TOPPING		
6	plum tomatoes, sliced	9
1 teaspoon	dried oregano	1½ teaspoons
1 teaspoon	dried thyme leaves	1½ teaspoons
1	garlic clove(s), minced	1½
8	canned anchovies, rinsed (optional)	12
¼ cup	grated Parmesan cheese	¼ cup plus 2 tablespoons

1. Add all ingredients for the dough in the order suggested by your bread machine manual and process on the dough cycle according to the manufacturer's directions.
2. At the end of the dough cycle remove the dough from the machine. Preheat the oven to 400 degrees. Divide the dough in half (thirds). On a floured board with a floured rolling pin, roll each piece of dough into a 10-inch circle and place on pizza pans or nonstick baking sheets.
3. Cover the dough with the tomato slices, leaving a 1-inch margin all around. Sprinkle the oregano, thyme, and garlic evenly over the pizzas. Arrange the anchovies on top, if you are using them, and sprinkle 2 tablespoons Parmesan cheese over each pizza. Bake 20 minutes, or until brown.

PER SERVING: 163 Calories; 1.5 gm. Fat; 2 mg. Cholesterol; 8% Calories from Fat

Mediterranean Vegetable Pizza

This low-fat version of classic pizza gives you lots of fiber and vitamins on a voluptuously topped, crisp pie.

Yield: 2 (10-inch) pizzas, 8 servings

DOUGH

1½ teaspoons	dry yeast
2 cups	bread flour
¼ cup	wheat bran
¾ teaspoon	salt
2 tablespoons	minced prunes*
¾ cup plus 2 tablespoons	water
1 tablespoon	yellow cornmeal

TOPPING

2	medium onions
1	medium zucchini
1	large tomato
4	garlic cloves
2 teaspoons	chopped fresh basil
½ teaspoon	dried oregano
½ teaspoon	dried thyme leaves

1. Add all ingredients for the dough except the cornmeal in the order suggested by your bread machine manual and process on the dough cycle according to the manufacturer's directions.

2. While the dough is being processed, preheat the oven to 450 degrees. Place the onions in their skins, the whole zucchini, the tomato, and the garlic cloves in their skins on a nonstick baking sheet. Bake the tomato and garlic 20 minutes, the onions and zucchini 40 minutes. Let the vegetables cool. Peel the onions and garlic. Chop the vegetables coarsely.

3. At the end of the dough cycle, remove the dough from the machine and divide it in half. On a floured board with a floured rolling pin, roll each piece of dough into a 10-inch round. Sprinkle the cornmeal on 2 nonstick baking sheets or pizza pans. Place the dough on the pans, prick all over with a fork, and bake 15 minutes. Top the pizzas with the chopped vegetables and bake 5 minutes longer. Remove the pizzas from the oven and sprinkle with the basil, oregano, and thyme on top. Eat hot or at room temperature.

*If the prunes are hard, pour boiling water over them to soften, then drain well.

PER SERVING: 171 Calories; .9 gm. Fat; 0 mg. Cholesterol; 5% Calories from Fat

Roasted Onion and Potato Bread

Burnished gold, roasted onion gives this bread the illusion of a richness that usually comes from butter or olive oil. Mashed potato makes the bread soft, and the crisp potato skin gives it crunch. This is one of our favorites.

SMALL LOAF (1 POUND)	INGREDIENTS	LARGE LOAF (1½ POUNDS)
1 medium	whole onion, with the skin intact	1 large
1 medium	baking potato, unpeeled	1 large
1 teaspoon	dry yeast	1½ teaspoons
1¾ cups	bread flour	2⅔ cups
½ cup	whole wheat flour	¾ cup
½ teaspoon	salt	¾ teaspoon
½ cup	water	¾ cup

1. Preheat the oven to 450 degrees. Roast the onion and potato 45 minutes. Cool. Discard the brown skin of the onion and chop the onion coarsely. Use ½ cup (¾ cup) for the bread; reserve the rest for another use. Cut the potato in half. Scoop out the potato and mash. Use ½ (¾) cup of mashed potato for the bread; reserve the rest for another recipe. Chop the potato skin coarsely and reserve.

2. Add all ingredients except the potato skin in the order suggested by your bread machine manual and process on the basic bread cycle according to the manufacturer's directions.

3. Add the chopped skin at the beeper or at the end of the first kneading in machines without a beeper to signal addition of fruit and nuts.

PER (1-OUNCE) SERVING: 77 Calories; .3 gm. Fat; 0 mg. Cholesterol; 4% Calories from Fat

Potato Bread Studded with Artichoke Hearts

As a first course, serve a slice of this artichoke enclosed in bread graced with a salsa or a puddle of thick, herbed tomato sauce. Slice carefully to keep the artichokes in place.

SMALL LOAF (1 POUND)	INGREDIENTS	LARGE LOAF (1½ POUNDS)
1 teaspoon	dry yeast	1½ teaspoons
1¾ cups	bread flour	2⅔ cups
½ cup	whole wheat flour	¾ cup
¼ cup	mashed potato	⅓ cup
2 tablespoons	wheat bran	3 tablespoons
½ teaspoon	salt	¾ teaspoon
⅛ teaspoon	freshly ground black pepper	¼ teaspoon
¾ cup plus 2 tablespoons	water	1½ cups
3	artichoke hearts, canned or thawed frozen	4

1. Add all ingredients except the artichoke hearts in the order suggested by your bread machine manual and process on the basic bread cycle according to the manufacturer's directions.

2. While the bread is being processed, drain the artichoke hearts and pat dry with paper towels. During the last rising, before the bread begins to bake, carefully press the artichoke hearts down the length of the dough, so that when the loaf is baked, the center of each slice of bread will contain a slice of artichoke. Close the bread machine and let the bread finish rising and baking. Let cool before slicing.

PER (1-OUNCE) SERVING: 74 Calories; .3 gm. Fat; 0 mg. Cholesterol; 4% Calories from Fat

Herbed Potato Turnovers

Using dough as the wrapper gives you a juicy, naturally sweet vegetable filling plus a crispy, herbed edible crust. This can be served as a first course or as a side dish with a fish entrée.

Yield: 8 turnovers, 8 servings

DOUGH

---

1 teaspoon	dry yeast
1½ cups	bread flour
¾ cup	whole wheat flour
1 teaspoon	dried thyme leaves
1 teaspoon	dried rosemary
½ teaspoon	salt
¼ cup	nonfat plain yogurt
¾ cup	water

FILLING

---

2 cups	cubed (½-inch) raw potatoes (preferably small red or Yukon gold)
2	garlic cloves, sliced
1 teaspoon	minced fresh rosemary or thyme leaves

1. Add all ingredients for the dough in the order suggested by your bread machine manual and process on the dough cycle according to the manufacturer's directions.
2. Preheat the oven to 400 degrees. At the end of the dough cycle, divide the

---

dough into 8 equal pieces. On a floured board with floured hands, press each piece of dough into a 6-inch round. Place equal portions of potato, garlic, and rosemary in the center of each round. Fold the edges of the dough over the filling to form turnovers; press the edges together tightly to seal.

3. Place the packets, seam sides-down, on a nonstick baking sheet, cover loosely, and let rise in a draft-free place 15 minutes. Bake 30 minutes, or until golden brown.

PER SERVING: 168 Calories; .7 gm. Fat; .1 mg. Cholesterol; 4% Calories from Fat

Provençal Bread

The earthy smells of garlic and thyme and the flavors of tomato and anise, emblems of the south of France, are what give this bread its assertive taste. Serve slices as an hors d'oeuvre or take it to the beach.

SMALL LOAF (1 POUND)	INGREDIENTS	LARGE LOAF (1½ POUNDS)
1 teaspoon	dry yeast	1½ teaspoons
1½ cups	bread flour	2¼ cups
¾ cup	whole wheat flour	1 cup plus 2 tablespoons
½ teaspoon	anise or fennel seeds	¾ teaspoon
1 teaspoon	dried thyme leaves	1½ teaspoons
1	garlic clove(s), minced	1½
¼ cup	chopped sun-dried tomatoes*	⅓ cup
½ teaspoon	salt	¾ teaspoon
¼ cup	minced onion	⅓ cup
¼ cup	mashed potato	⅓ cup
⅔ cup	water	1 cup

Add all ingredients in the order suggested by your bread machine manual and process on the basic bread cycle according to the manufacturer's directions.

*Pour boiling water over the sun-dried tomato halves. Soak 10 minutes, drain, and cool to room temperature. With a scissors, snip into ¼-inch pieces. Do not use tomatoes that are reconstituted and packed in oil for this recipe.

PER (1-OUNCE) SERVING: 74 Calories; .4 gm. Fat; 0 mg. Cholesterol; 4% Calories from Fat

Russian Pumpernickel

Cut this bread thin and cover with smoked fish or sliced radishes or with horseradish mixed with yogurt topped by a paper-thin slice of cold, lean roast beef or raw tuna.

SMALL LOAF (1 POUND)	INGREDIENTS	LARGE LOAF (1½ POUNDS)
1¼ teaspoons	dry yeast	1¾ teaspoons
2 cups	bread flour	3 cups
½ cup	rye flour	¾ cup
½ teaspoon	salt	¾ teaspoon
1 teaspoon	caramel coloring (optional)*	1½ teaspoons
¼ cup	grated raw potato	⅓ cup
¼ cup	sourdough starter**	⅓ cup
¾ cup	water	1 cup

Add all ingredients in the order suggested by your bread machine manual and process on the basic bread cycle according to the manufacturer's directions.

*See mail-order sources on page 12. If the caramel coloring is omitted, the bread will not be dark, but the flavor will be the same.
**After measuring out what is needed for this recipe, be sure to replenish your sourdough starter with equal amounts of flour and water.

PER (1-OUNCE) SERVING: 80 Calories; .3 gm. Fat; 0 mg. Cholesterol; 4% Calories from Fat

Pumpkin and Sweet Apple Bread

SMALL LOAF (1 POUND)	INGREDIENTS	LARGE LOAF (1½ POUNDS)
1 teaspoon	dry yeast	1½ teaspoons
1¾ cups	bread flour	2⅔ cups
½ cup	whole wheat flour	¾ cup
2 tablespoons	nonfat dry milk	3 tablespoons
2 tablespoons	rolled oats	3 tablespoons
1 teaspoon	ground cinnamon	1½ teaspoons
½ teaspoon	ground ginger	¾ teaspoon
¼ teaspoon	ground cloves	½ teaspoon
½ teaspoon	salt	¾ teaspoon
½ cup	canned or fresh pumpkin puree	¾ cup
¼ cup	apple juice concentrate, thawed	⅓ cup
⅓ cup	water	½ cup
½ cup	chopped dried apples	¾ cup

1. Add all ingredients except the dried apples in the order suggested by your bread machine manual and process on the basic bread cycle according to the manufacturer's directions.

2. Add the apples at the beeper or at the end of the first kneading in machines without a beeper to signal addition of fruit and nuts.

PER (1-OUNCE) SERVING: 91 Calories; .4 gm. Fat; .1 mg. Cholesterol; 4% Calories from Fat

Sweet Pumpkin and Oat Bread

Make canapés of this bread with smoked turkey and chutney or cucumber and corn salsa. Leftover bread makes a slightly sweet and spicy stuffing for chicken.

SMALL LOAF (1 POUND)	INGREDIENTS	LARGE LOAF (1½ POUNDS)
1¼ teaspoons	dry yeast	2 teaspoons
1¾ cups	bread flour	2⅔ cups
½ cup	whole wheat flour	¾ cup
¼ cup	rolled oats	⅓ cup
2 tablespoons	nonfat dry milk	3 tablespoons
1 teaspoon	minced fresh ginger	1½ teaspoons
1 teaspoon	grated orange zest	1½ teaspoons
½ teaspoon	salt	¾ teaspoon
¾ cup	pumpkin puree	1 cup plus 2 tablespoons
½ cup	water	¾ cup
¼ cup	currants or raisins	⅓ cup

1. Add all ingredients except the currants in the order suggested by your bread machine manual and process on the basic bread cycle according to the manufacturer's directions.

2. Add the currants at the beeper or at the end of the first kneading in machines without a beeper to signal addition of fruit and nuts.

PER (1-OUNCE) SERVING: 83 Calories; .4 gm. Fat; .1 mg. Cholesterol; 4% Calories from Fat

Quinoa, Basil, and Sun-Dried Tomato Bread

When you crave an hors d'oeuvre with the flavor of the Eastern Mediterranean, serve this herbed quinoa bread with a yogurt dip, eggplant caviar, or hummus.

SMALL LOAF (1 POUND)	INGREDIENTS	LARGE LOAF (1½ POUNDS)
1½ teaspoons	dry yeast	2¼ teaspoons
2 cups	bread flour	3 cups
2 tablespoons	wheat bran	3 tablespoons
¼ cup	quinoa grain	⅓ cup
2 tablespoons	nonfat dry milk	3 tablespoons
2 teaspoons	dried basil	1 tablespoon
¼ cup	chopped sun-dried tomatoes*	⅓ cup
¾ teaspoon	salt	1 teaspoon
¾ cup plus 2 tablespoons	water	1¼ cups

Add all ingredients in the order suggested by your bread machine manual and process on the basic bread cycle according to the manufacturer's directions.

*Pour boiling water over sun-dried tomato halves. Soak 10 minutes, drain, and cool to room temperature. With a scissors, snip into ¼-inch pieces. Do not use tomatoes that are reconstituted and packed in oil for this recipe.

PER (1-OUNCE) SERVING: 80 Calories; .5 gm. Fat; .1 mg. Cholesterol; 5% Calories from Fat

Quinoa, Yogurt, and Orange Bread

On a summer afternoon at your vacation cottage, it is too hot to cook. For breakfast, lunch, or tea on the porch, toast this fruity bread and slice very ripe strawberries or peaches on top. Add a dab of yogurt cheese. It keeps well, too.

SMALL LOAF (1 POUND)	INGREDIENTS	LARGE LOAF (1½ POUNDS)
1¼ teaspoons	dry yeast	2 teaspoons
2 cups	bread flour	3 cups
¼ cup	quinoa grain	⅓ cup
2 tablespoons	wheat bran	3 tablespoons
1 tablespoon	grated orange zest	1½ tablespoons
1 tablespoon	minced prunes*	1½ tablespoons
¼ cup	nonfat plain yogurt	⅓ cup
½ teaspoon	salt	¾ teaspoon
¾ cup	water	1 cup plus 2 tablespoons

Add all ingredients in the order suggested by your bread machine manual and process on the basic bread cycle according to the manufacturer's directions.

*If the prunes are hard, pour boiling water over them to soften, then drain well.

PER (1-OUNCE) SERVING: 78 Calories; .4 gm. Fat; .1 mg. Cholesterol; 5% Calories from Fat

Salsa Bread

This is a lively hors d'oeuvre with beer or iced tea. Freeze leftovers, slice very thin, and toast in the oven or toaster oven. Serve these chip-like snacks with chopped tomato and cilantro or baby salad greens with vinaigrette dressing.

SMALL LOAF (1 POUND)	INGREDIENTS	LARGE LOAF (1½ POUNDS)
1 teaspoon	dry yeast	1½ teaspoons
2 cups	bread flour	3 cups
¼ cup	whole wheat flour	⅓ cup
¼ cup	chopped sun-dried tomatoes*	⅓ cup
1 teaspoon	ground coriander	1½ teaspoons
2 teaspoons	minced fresh jalapeño pepper or ¼ teaspoon crushed hot pepper	1 tablespoon
1	garlic clove(s), minced	1½
½ teaspoon	salt	¾ teaspoon
¾ cup plus 2 tablespoons	water	1¼ cups

Add all ingredients in the order suggested by your bread machine manual and process on the basic bread cycle according to the manufacturer's directions.

*Pour boiling water over the sun-dried tomato halves. Soak 10 minutes, drain, and cool to room temperature. With a scissors, snip into ¼-inch pieces. Do not use tomatoes that are reconstituted and packed in oil for this recipe.

PER (1-OUNCE) SERVING: 73 Calories; .4 gm. Fat; 0 mg. Cholesterol; 4% Calories from Fat

Salsa Verde Bread

Since the flavor sings out in this bread, sandwich fillings can be low-key yet crunchy. If you have a julienne blade on your food processor, cut a pile of radishes, celery, carrots, zucchini, and turnips and pile them on slices of Salsa Verde Bread.

SMALL LOAF (1 POUND)	INGREDIENTS	LARGE LOAF (1½ POUNDS)
1 teaspoon	dry yeast	1½ teaspoons
2 cups	bread flour	3 cups
2 tablespoons	wheat bran	3 tablespoons
1	garlic clove(s), minced	2
½ cup (packed)	minced fresh parsley	¾ cup (packed)
1 tablespoon	capers, rinsed and drained	1½ tablespoons
2 tablespoons	minced prunes*	3 tablespoons
½ teaspoon	salt	¾ teaspoon
⅔ cup	water	1 cup

Add all ingredients in the order suggested by your bread machine manual and process on the basic bread cycle according to the manufacturer's directions.

*If the prunes are hard, pour boiling water over them to soften, then drain well.

PER (1-OUNCE) SERVING: 68 Calories; .3 gm. Fat; 0 mg. Cholesterol; 4% Calories from Fat

Sicilian Bread

Sicilians make a pasta sauce out of capers, currants, and tomato. Kneading all of these assertive tastes into a bread adds up to a complex loaf, spicy enough to eat on its own.

SMALL LOAF (1 POUND)	INGREDIENTS	LARGE LOAF (1½ POUNDS)
1½ teaspoons	dry yeast	2¼ teaspoons
1¾ cups	bread flour	2⅔ cups
½ cup	whole wheat flour	¾ cup
⅛ teaspoon	freshly ground black pepper	¼ teaspoon
2 tablespoons	capers	3 tablespoons
1 tablespoon	red wine vinegar	1½ tablespoons
½ teaspoon	salt	¾ teaspoon
2 tablespoons	currants or raisins	3 tablespoons
2 tablespoons	chopped sun-dried tomatoes*	3 tablespoons
¾ cup	water	1 cup plus 2 tablespoons

Add all ingredients in the order suggested by your bread machine manual and process on the basic bread cycle according to the manufacturer's directions.

*Pour boiling water over the sun-dried tomato halves. Soak 10 minutes, drain, and cool to room temperature. With a scissors, snip into ¼-inch pieces. Do not use tomatoes that are reconstituted and packed in oil for this recipe.

PER (1-OUNCE) SERVING: 72 Calories; .3 gm. Fat; 0 mg. Cholesterol; 4% Calories from Fat

Spinach and Potato Bread

Potato softens this bread; black pepper makes it bold but not overly assertive. Serve as an hors d'oeuvre with hummus or a dip made of yogurt cheese and sun-dried tomatoes.

SMALL LOAF (1 POUND)	INGREDIENTS	LARGE LOAF (1½ POUNDS)
1 (10-ounce) package	frozen chopped spinach, thawed	1 (10-ounce) package
1 teaspoon	dry yeast	1½ teaspoons
1¾ cups	bread flour	2⅔ cups
½ cup	whole wheat flour	¾ cup
2 tablespoons	nonfat dry milk	3 tablespoons
½ teaspoon	salt	¾ teaspoon
⅛ teaspoon	freshly ground black pepper	¼ teaspoon
¼ cup	grated raw potato (no need to remove the skin)	⅓ cup
½ cup	water	¾ cup

1. Squeeze the spinach to remove as much water as possible. Measure out ½ (¾) cup for this recipe. Reserve the rest for another use.

2. Add all ingredients in the order suggested by your bread machine manual and process on the basic bread cycle according to the manufacturer's directions.

PER (1-OUNCE) SERVING: 73 Calories; .3 gm. Fat; .1 mg. Cholesterol; 4% Calories from Fat

Spinach and Sun-Dried Tomato Bread

SMALL LOAF (1 POUND)	INGREDIENTS	LARGE LOAF (1½ POUNDS)
1 (10-ounce) package	frozen chopped spinach, thawed	1 (10-ounce) package
1¼ teaspoons	dry yeast	2 teaspoons
1¾ cups	bread flour	2⅔ cups
½ cup	whole wheat flour	¾ cup
¼ cup	chopped sun-dried tomatoes*	⅓ cup
¼ cup	minced onions	⅓ cup
1 teaspoon	dried oregano	1½ teaspoons
½ teaspoon	salt	¾ teaspoon
2	egg whites	3
⅓ cup	water	½ cup

1. Squeeze the spinach to remove as much water as possible. Measure out ½ (¾) cup for this recipe. Reserve the rest for another use.

2. Add all ingredients in the order suggested by your bread machine manual and process on the basic bread cycle according to the manufacturer's directions.

*Pour boiling water over the sun-dried tomato halves. Soak 10 minutes, drain, and let cool to room temperature. With a scissors, snip into ¼-inch pieces. Do not use tomatoes that are reconstituted and packed in oil for this recipe

PER (1-OUNCE) SERVING: 77 Calories; .4 gm. Fat; 0 mg. Cholesterol; 4% Calories from Fat

Stuffing Bread

As the demands of the holidays overwhelm you, getting the turkey ready will be the easiest part. Make this bread, complete with all the classic seasonings, weeks ahead (and freeze it) or a day ahead. Cut it into cubes and stuff it into the bird. A 1-pound loaf should fill a big chicken or small turkey. Use one large or two small loaves for a 15- to 20-pound turkey. Or serve slices separately to sop up the juices.

SMALL LOAF (1 POUND)	INGREDIENTS	LARGE LOAF (1½ POUNDS)
1 teaspoon	dry yeast	1½ teaspoons
1¾ cups	bread flour	2⅔ cups
½ cup	whole wheat flour	¾ cup
2 teaspoons	dried onion flakes	1 tablespoon
1	garlic clove(s), minced	1½
2 teaspoons	dried sage	1 tablespoon
¼ teaspoon	freshly ground black pepper	¼ teaspoon
½ teaspoon	salt	¾ teaspoon
¾ cup plus 2 tablespoons	water	1¼ cups

Add all ingredients in the order suggested by your bread machine manual and process on the basic bread cycle according to the manufacturer's directions.

PER (1-OUNCE) SERVING: 69 Calories; .3 gm. Fat; 0 mg. Cholesterol; 4% Calories from Fat

Tandoori Vegetable Tart

This spicy tart can be an hors d'oeuvre or the better part of lunch or a light supper along with lentil soup or consommé. Pass yogurt and serve beer or hot tea with it in the late afternoon.

Yield: 2 (10-inch) tarts, 6 servings each

DOUGH

1¼ teaspoons	dry yeast
2 cups	bread flour
¼ cup	wheat bran
½ teaspoon	salt
¾ cup plus 2 tablespoons	water

TOPPING

2 tablespoons	nonfat plain yogurt
1 tablespoon	lemon juice
1½ teaspoons	garam masala*
1 teaspoon	ground ginger
¼ teaspoon	turmeric
⅛ teaspoon	cayenne
1	garlic clove, minced
4	medium potatoes, sliced paper thin
2	medium onions, sliced paper thin

1. Add all ingredients for the dough in the order suggested by your bread machine manual and process on the dough cycle according to the manufacturer's directions.

2. Meanwhile, in a small bowl, mix together the yogurt, lemon juice, garam masala, ginger, turmeric, cayenne, and garlic.

3. Place the potatoes in a medium saucepan with cold water to cover. Bring to a boil; drain. Separate the onion slices into rings.

4. At the end of the dough cycle, remove the dough from the machine and divide in half. On a floured board with a floured rolling pin, roll each piece into a 10-inch circle. Place on a nonstick baking sheet(s). Paint with yogurt mixture. Let rise in a draft-free place 20 minutes.

5. While the crust is rising, preheat the oven to 450 degrees. Bake the crusts for 10 minutes. Remove from the oven, turn over, and paint with the rest of the yogurt mixture. If the crust has puffed too much in the oven, carefully prick it to release some steam. Arrange the potatoes over the crust. Add the onion rings and bake 15 minutes.

*Garam masala is an Indian spice mixture. If it is not available, make your own from equal parts of ground cumin, coriander, cardamom, cinnamon, black pepper, and cloves.

PER SERVING: 145 Calories; .6 gm. Fat; .1 mg. Cholesterol; 4% Calories from Fat

Wheatberry Cranberry Bread

Bright cranberries stud every slice of this moist bread with burnished fall red. The wheatberries and oats add nutty taste and texture without fat.

SMALL LOAF (1 POUND)	INGREDIENTS	LARGE LOAF (1½ POUNDS)
1 teaspoon	dry yeast	1½ teaspoons
2 cups	bread flour	3 cups
2 tablespoons	rolled oats	3 tablespoons
2 tablespoons	nonfat dry milk	3 tablespoons
½ teaspoon	salt	¾ teaspoon
¼ cup	minced prunes*	⅓ cup
½ cup	cooked wheatberries (see page 5)	¾ cup
⅔ cup	water	1 cup
½ cup	fresh cranberries	¾ cup

1. Add all ingredients except the cranberries in the order suggested by your bread machine manual and process on the basic bread cycle according to the manufacturer's directions.

2. Add the cranberries at the beeper or at the end of the first kneading in machines without a beeper to signal addition of fruit and nuts.

*If the prunes are hard, pour boiling water over them to soften, then drain well.

PER (1-OUNCE) SERVING: 84 Calories; .4 gm. Fat; .1 mg. Cholesterol; 5% Calories from Fat

Jalapeño Whole Wheat Bread

This easy hors d'oeuvre is not as spicy as it sounds and is instantly turned into open-faced sandwiches with a slice of tomato and a sprinkle of chopped cilantro.

SMALL LOAF (1 POUND)	INGREDIENTS	LARGE LOAF (1½ POUNDS)
1¼ teaspoons	dry yeast	2 teaspoons
1½ cups	bread flour	2¼ cups
¾ cup	whole wheat flour	1 cup plus 2 tablespoons
1 teaspoon	vital wheat gluten*	1½ teaspoons
½ teaspoon	salt	¾ teaspoon
¼ cup	yellow cornmeal	⅓ cup
1 tablespoon	minced fresh jalapeño pepper(s)	1½ tablespoons
1	garlic clove(s), minced	1½
¼ cup	mashed banana	⅓ cup
1	egg white(s)	2
⅔ cup	water	¾ cup plus 2 tablespoons

Add all ingredients in the order suggested by your bread machine manual and process on the basic bread cycle according to the manufacturer's directions.

*Vital wheat gluten is available at health food stores.

PER (1-OUNCE) SERVING: 79 Calories; .4 gm. Fat; 0 mg. Cholesterol; 5% Calories from Fat

Gingered Yogurt and Banana Bread

For a warming snack with hot cider or cocoa or a glass of port, this bread is just sweet enough either toasted or plain. It is airy and slightly spicy and has a good "tear" (rhymes with bare), that desirable elastic quality.

SMALL LOAF (1 POUND)	INGREDIENTS	LARGE LOAF (1½ POUNDS)
1¼ teaspoons	dry yeast	2 teaspoons
2 cups	bread flour	3 cups
2 tablespoons	wheat bran	3 tablespoons
2 tablespoons	wheat germ	3 tablespoons
2 tablespoons	nonfat dry milk	3 tablespoons
1 teaspoon	ground ginger	1½ teaspoons
¾ teaspoon	salt	1 teaspoon
¼ cup	mashed banana	⅓ cup
¼ cup	nonfat plain yogurt	⅓ cup
½ cup	water	¾ cup

Add all ingredients in the order suggested by your bread machine manual and process on the basic bread cycle according to the manufacturer's directions.

PER (1-OUNCE) SERVING: 75 Calories; .4 gm. Fat; .2 mg. Cholesterol; 5% Calories from Fat

Zucchini and Roasted Pepper Bread

Half the flavor of a hero sandwich is baked into this bread. Add shredded lettuce and sliced tomato and perhaps a very thin slice of lean prosciutto for a sandwich with much gusto but little fat.

SMALL LOAF (1 POUND)	INGREDIENTS	LARGE LOAF (1½ POUNDS)
1 teaspoon	dry yeast	1½ teaspoons
1¾ cups	bread flour	2⅔ cups
½ cup	whole wheat flour	¾ cup
1	garlic clove(s), minced	1½
½ teaspoon	salt	¾ teaspoon
2 tablespoons	minced prunes*	3 tablespoons
1 cup	grated zucchini	1½ cups
2 tablespoons	minced roasted red peppers or pimientos	3 tablespoons
¼ cup	water	⅓ cup plus 1 tablespoon

Add all ingredients in the order suggested by your bread machine manual and process on the basic bread cycle according to the manufacturer's directions.

*If the prunes are hard, pour boiling water over them to soften, then drain well.

PER (1-OUNCE) SERVING: 72 Calories; .3 gm. Fat; 0 mg. Cholesterol; 4% Calories from Fat

Chapter Four

Salt-Free Breads

The bread machine is precious to people who need or simply prefer to eat salt-free breads and who eschew salt substitutes. The machine makes it easy to do the baking and to control the ingredients, which really do matter when you omit all salt.

Even though salt makes up less than one percent of the total ingredients in an average loaf of bread and is often not perceived in taste, the influence salt has on the bread is enormous.

Salt has three functions in bread baking. It inhibits the yeast, slowing and controlling the rising so that air bubbles are not too big and the dough doesn't overrise and deflate. It heightens the taste of the bread and intensifies the flavor of other ingredients. And it acts as a preservative, keeping the loaf fresh a little longer.

Creating this chapter of sugar-free, low-fat breads without any salt at all was a tremendous challenge. To begin with, I used less yeast in the recipes in this chapter to make up for the absence of salt. No need for preservatives since you are making the bread just in time to eat it at its freshest. To keep the flavors strong, I added larger-than-usual proportions of dried fruits, herbs, and spices. Since the breads are so fresh, the flavor will be at its peak.

Salt-Free Fruited Foccacia

Yield: 1 foccacia, 8 servings

2 teaspoons	dry yeast
2 tablespoons	nonfat dry milk
2 cups	bread flour
¾ cup	water
½ cup	raisins
½ cup	dried cherries
2 tablespoons	orange juice

1. In a small bowl, combine the yeast, dry milk, ½ cup of the bread flour, and the water. Mix well. Cover and let this sponge rise in a draft-free place ½ hour.

2. Add the remaining 1½ cups bread flour, the sponge, and ¼ cup each of the raisins and dried cherries in the order suggested by your bread machine manual and process on the dough cycle according to the manufacturer's directions.

3. While the dough is processing, mix together the remaining raisins and dried cherries and the orange juice for the topping. Preheat the oven to 375 degrees.

4. When the dough cycle ends, remove the dough from the machine. On a floured board with a floured rolling pin, roll the dough into a 12-inch circle. Place on a nonstick baking sheet. If it overhangs the sheet, don't worry. Sprinkle the filling on top, leaving a 3-inch border all around. Fold the edges toward the center to completely cover the cherries and raisins. Cover and let rise in a draft-free place ½ hour. Bake the foccacia 20 minutes, or until golden. Cut into 8 wedges to serve.

PER SERVING: 187 Calories; .6 gm. Fat; .2 mg. Cholesterol; 3% Calories from Fat

Salt-Free Bagels

If possible, make the dough the night before, refrigerate, and finish in the morning for hot bagels for breakfast. Slice and spread with yogurt cheese or with mashed ripe mango or banana.

Yield: 8 bagels, 8 servings

1¼ teaspoons	dry yeast
1¾ cups	bread flour
½ cup	whole wheat flour
2 tablespoons	apple butter (no sugar added)
4 teaspoons	dried minced onion
¾ cup	water
1 tablespoon	barley malt syrup (optional)*

1. Add all ingredients for the dough except the barley malt syrup and 2 teaspoons of the minced onion in the order suggested by your bread machine manual and process on the dough cycle according to the manufacturer's directions.
2. At the end of the dough cycle, remove the dough from the machine. Preheat the oven to 375 degrees. In a large pot, bring 2 quarts of water to a boil.
3. Divide the dough into 8 equal pieces. Roll each piece into a rope about 10 inches long. Make a circle of each piece, overlapping the ends by at least 1 inch and pressing or rolling the overlap tightly to seal. Let the bagels rise only 5 minutes.
4. Add the malt syrup, if using, to the boiling water. Lower a few bagels at a time into the boiling water. As soon as the bagels rise to the top, remove with a skimmer or spatula to a nonstick baking sheet. Sprinkle with the remaining 2 teaspoons minced onions and bake 20 minutes, or until golden.

*Barley malt syrup is available at some health food stores or can be mail-ordered from sources on page 12. It gives the bagels their shiny golden crust, but if it is omitted, the flavor will be almost the same.

PER SERVING: 149 Calories; 1 gm. Fat; 0 mg. Cholesterol; 4% Calories from Fat

Salt-Free Cornmeal and Fennel Bread

This moist, aromatic bread is fine as a canapé with a dab of salsa or smoked trout or layered with lots of greens and very thin slices of orange for a refreshing yet filling sandwich.

SMALL LOAF (1 POUND)	INGREDIENTS	LARGE LOAF (1½ POUNDS)
SPONGE		
½ cup	sourdough starter*	¾ cup
⅓ cup	water	½ cup
½ cup	yellow cornmeal	¾ cup
½ cup	bread flour	¾ cup
DOUGH		
¾ teaspoon	dry yeast	1¼ teaspoons
1¼ cups	bread flour	1¾ cups plus 2 tablespoons
½ cup	whole wheat flour	¾ cup
¼ cup	mashed banana	⅓ cup
1 teaspoon	fennel seeds	1½ teaspoons
1 teaspoon	grated orange zest	1½ teaspoons
⅓ cup	water	½ cup

1. Prepare the sponge: In a medium bowl, mix together the sourdough starter, ⅓ cup (½ cup) water, cornmeal, and ½ cup (¾ cup) flour until well blended. Cover this sponge and let rest 1 hour.

2. Add all ingredient in the order suggested by your bread machine manual and process on the basic bread cycle according to the manufacturer's directions. Include the sponge with the liquid ingredients.

*After measuring out what is needed for this recipe, be sure to replenish your sourdough starter with equal amounts of flour and water.

PER (1-OUNCE) SERVING: 94 Calories; .4 gm. Fat; 0 mg. Cholesterol; 4% Calories from Fat

Salt-Free Mandelbrot

This Eastern European version of a biscotti is for dunking in coffee. Keep in a tin for ready snacks to serve with fruit salads or compotes.

SMALL LOAF (1 POUND)	INGREDIENTS	LARGE LOAF (1½ POUNDS)
1 teaspoon	dry yeast	1½ teaspoons
1¾ cups	bread flour	2⅔ cups
½ cup	whole wheat flour	¾ cup
Pinch	baking soda	⅛ teaspoon
1 tablespoon	grated orange zest	1½ tablespoons
1 teaspoon	vanilla extract	1½ teaspoons
2 tablespoons	apple butter (no sugar added)	3 tablespoons
2 tablespoons	minced dried figs*	3 tablespoons
¾ cup	water	1 cup plus 2 tablespoons
¼ cup	coarsely chopped almonds	⅓ cup
½ cup	raisins	¾ cup

1. Add all ingredients except the almonds and raisins according to your bread machine manual and process on the basic bread cycle according to the manufacturer's directions.

2. Add the almonds and raisins at the beeper or at the end of the first kneading in machines without a beeper to signal addition of fruit and nuts.

3. At the end of the baking cycle, remove the bread from the machine and cool. It is preferable to let the bread get stale for a day. Preheat the oven to 300 degrees.

Cut the bread into ½-inch-thick slices. Cut each slice into ½-inch fingers. Bake 1 hour, or until lightly golden.

*If the figs are hard, pour boiling water over them to soften, then drain well.

PER (1-OUNCE) SERVING: 100 Calories; 1.4 gm. Fat; 0 mg. Cholesterol; 12% Calories from fat

Salt-Free Multigrain Bread

Loaded with protein, fiber, and vitamins, this is a truly nutritious bread. Cool completely, then slice thin for sandwiches laced with cheese and sliced grapes or grilled fennel and thinly sliced, peeled orange.

SMALL LOAF (1 POUND)	INGREDIENTS	LARGE LOAF (1½ POUNDS)
1¼ teaspoons	dry yeast	2 teaspoons
2 cups	bread flour	3 cups
2 tablespoons	nonfat dry milk	3 tablespoons
2 tablespoons	wheat bran	3 tablespoons
2 tablespoons	amaranth flour	3 tablespoons
2 tablespoons	rolled oats	3 tablespoons
2 tablespoons	rye flour	3 tablespoons
2 teaspoons	grated orange zest	1 tablespoon
1 tablespoon	barley malt syrup (optional)*	1½ tablespoons
¾ cup plus 2 tablespoons	water	1¼ cups

Add all ingredients in the order suggested by your bread machine manual and process on the basic bread cycle according to the manufacturer's directions.

NOTE: To keep whole-grain products, such as wheat bran and rye flour fresh, be sure to store them in a tightly covered container in the freezer.

*Barley malt syrup is available at some health food stores or by mail order from sources listed on page 12. If it is omitted, the bread will be lighter in color, but the flavor will be almost the same.

PER (1-OUNCE) SERVING: 77 Calories; .5 gm. Fat; .1 mg. Cholesterol; 5% Calories from Fat

Salt-Free Orange Bread

This moist, almost nutty bread makes fine sandwiches filled with Waldorf salad (apples, raisins, and celery), watercress and tuna, or artichoke hearts with a sprinkle of Parmesan cheese.

SMALL LOAF (1 POUND)	INGREDIENTS	LARGE LOAF (1½ POUNDS)
¾ teaspoon	dry yeast	1 teaspoon
1½ cups	bread flour	2¼ cups
¾ cup	whole wheat flour	1 cup plus 2 tablespoons
3 tablespoons	nonfat dry milk	¼ cup
1 tablespoon	grated orange zest	1½ tablespoons
2 tablespoons	apple butter (no sugar added)	3 tablespoons
¾ cup plus 2 tablespoons	water	1¼ cups

Add all ingredients in the order suggested by your bread machine manual and process on the basic bread cycle according to the manufacturer's directions.

PER (1-OUNCE) SERVING: 71 Calories; .3 gm. Fat; .1 mg. Cholesterol; 4% Calories from Fat

Salt-Free Potato and Dill Bread

Serve this subtly flavored bread alongside chowders or vegetable soups. For a sandwich in summer, fill with cold fish salad and a layer of sliced cucumber.

SMALL LOAF (1 POUND)	INGREDIENTS	LARGE LOAF (1½ POUNDS)
1 teaspoon	dry yeast	1½ teaspoons
1¼ cups	bread flour	1¾ cups plus 2 tablespoons
1 cup	whole wheat flour	1½ cups
2 tablespoons	nonfat dry milk	3 tablespoons
¼ cup	grated raw potato	⅓ cup
1 teaspoon	dill seeds	1½ teaspoons
1 teaspoon	dried dill weed	1½ teaspoons
½ teaspoon	caraway seeds	¾ teaspoon
¾ cup	water	1 cup plus 2 tablespoons

Add all ingredients in the order suggested by your bread machine manual and process on the basic bread cycle according to the manufacturer's directions.

PER (1-OUNCE) SERVING: 69 Calories; .4 gm. Fat; .1 mg. Cholesterol; 5% Calories from Fat

Salt-Free Pumpernickel

This is a classic sandwich bread to fill with tuna or with yogurt cheese and sliced seedless grapes or sliced pears or with tomato and watercress.

SMALL LOAF (1 POUND)	INGREDIENTS	LARGE LOAF (1½ POUNDS)
1 teaspoon	dry yeast	1½ teaspoons
1½ cups	bread flour	2¼ cups
½ cup	rye flour	¾ cup
½ cup	whole wheat flour	¾ cup
2 tablespoons	minced prunes*	3 tablespoons
1 teaspoon	caramel coloring (optional)**	1½ teaspoons
¾ cup plus 2 tablespoons	water	1¼ cups

Add all ingredients in the order suggested by your bread machine manual and process on the basic bread cycle according to the manufacturer's directions.

*If the prunes are hard, pour boiling water over them to soften, then drain well.
**Caramel coloring is available by mail from the sources listed on page 12. If it is omitted, the bread will be lighter in color, but the flavor will be the same.

PER (1-OUNCE) SERVING: 74 Calories; .3 gm. Fat; 0 mg. Cholesterol; 4% Calories from Fat

Salt-Free Rye with Roasted Onion and Thyme

Roasted onions and thyme lend this bread supple texture and woodsy fragrance. Serve a slice with grilled mushrooms or make a sandwich filled with turkey, sliced crisp radishes, bell pepper, and celery.

SMALL LOAF (1 POUND)	INGREDIENTS	LARGE LOAF (1½ POUNDS)
⅔ cup	chopped roasted onion*	1 cup
1 teaspoon	dry yeast	1½ teaspoons
2 cups	bread flour	3 cups
½ cup	rye flour	¾ cup
2 teaspoons	dried thyme leaves	1 tablespoon
½ cup	water	¾ cup

Add all ingredients in the order suggested by your bread machine manual and process on the basic bread cycle according to the manufacturer's directions.

*To roast the onion, preheat the oven to 450 degrees. Do not peel the onion. Place on a nonstick baking sheet and roast 45 to 60 minutes, until brown and soft. Peel when cool, then chop.

PER (1-OUNCE) SERVING: 67 Calories; .3 gm. Fat; 0 mg. Cholesterol; 4% Calories from Fat

Salt-Free Spinach and Yogurt Bread

This spicy bread threaded with green makes a fine hors d'oeuvre with a plain, cool yogurt dip and a drink—either lemonade, beer, or mint tea.

SMALL LOAF (1 POUND)	INGREDIENTS	LARGE LOAF (1½ POUNDS)
1 (10-ounce) package	frozen chopped spinach, thawed	1 (10-ounce) package
¾ teaspoon	dry yeast	1¼ teaspoons
1½ cups	bread flour	2¼ cups
¾ cup	whole wheat flour	1 cup plus 2 tablespoons
2 teaspoons	dried minced onion	1 tablespoon
¼ teaspoon	ground black pepper	½ teaspoon
½	garlic clove, minced	1
1 teaspoon	grated nutmeg	1½ teaspoons
¼ cup	nonfat plain yogurt	⅓ cup
1	egg white(s)	2
⅓ cup	water	½ cup

1. Squeeze the spinach to remove as much water as possible. Measure out ½ cup (¾ cup) for this recipe. Save the rest for another use.

2. Add all ingredients, including the spinach, in the order suggested by your bread machine manual and process on the basic bread cycle according to the manufacturer's directions.

PER (1-OUNCE) SERVING: 72 Calories; .4 gm. Fat; .1 mg. Cholesterol; 5% Calories from Fat

Salt-Free Winter Squash Bread

This is sweet enough for an afternoon pick-me-up, but not too sweet for breakfast. It is so luxuriant with its spicy savor that you will not miss the salt.

SMALL LOAF (1 POUND)	INGREDIENTS	LARGE LOAF (1½ POUNDS)
¾ teaspoon	dry yeast	1¼ teaspoons
1¾ cups	bread flour	2⅔ cups
½ cup	whole wheat flour	¾ cup
1 tablespoon	apple butter (no sugar added)	1½ tablespoons
1 teaspoon	ground cinnamon	1½ teaspoons
1 teaspoon	ground ginger	1½ teaspoons
½ cup	baked and mashed acorn or butternut squash or pumpkin puree	¾ cup
⅔ cup	water	1 cup
½ cup	currants or raisins	¾ cup

1. Add all ingredients except the currants or raisins in the order suggested by your bread machine manual and process on the basic bread cycle according to the manufacturer's directions.

2. Add the currants or raisins at the beeper or at the end of the first kneading in machines without a beeper to signal addition of fruit and nuts.

PER (1-OUNCE) SERVING: 85 Calories; .3 gm. Fat; 0 mg. Cholesterol; 3% Calories from Fat

Salt-Free Sourdough White Bread

Make this into any kind of sandwich or toast it and spread with sugar-free jam or mashed ripe fruit for breakfast.

SMALL LOAF (1 POUND)	INGREDIENTS	LARGE LOAF (1½ POUNDS)
1 teaspoon	dry yeast	1½ teaspoons
2 cups	bread flour	3 cups
2 tablespoons	mashed ripe banana	3 tablespoons
¼ cup	sourdough starter*	⅓ cup
⅔ cup	water	¾ cup plus 2 tablespoons

Add all ingredients in the order suggested by your bread machine manual and process on the basic bread cycle according to the manufacturer's directions.

*After measuring out what is needed for this recipe, be sure to replenish your sourdough starter with equal amounts of flour and water.

PER (1-OUNCE) SERVING: 69 Calories; .3 gm. Fat; 0 mg. Cholesterol; 4% Calories from Fat

Salt-Free Whole Wheat Bread

This bread tastes better cool. Slice it thin for breakfast with a smear of pot cheese or yogurt cheese or jam.

SMALL LOAF (1 POUND)	INGREDIENTS	LARGE LOAF (1½ POUNDS)
¾ teaspoon	dry yeast	1¼ teaspoons
1¼ cups	bread flour	2 cups
1 cup	whole wheat flour	1½ cups
2 tablespoons	nonfat dry milk	3 tablespoons
1 tablespoon	minced prunes*	1½ tablespoons
2 teaspoons	vital wheat gluten**	1 tablespoon
2 tablespoons	apple butter (no sugar added)	3 tablespoons
¾ cup	water	1 cup plus 2 tablespoons

Add all ingredients in the order suggested by your bread machine manual and process on the basic bread cycle according to the manufacturer's directions.

*If the prunes are hard, pour boiling water over them to soften, then drain well.
**Vital wheat gluten is available at health food stores.

PER (1-OUNCE) SERVING: 72 Calories; .3 gm. Fat; .1 mg. Cholesterol; 4% Calories from Fat

Chapter Five

Dessert Breads

The collection of recipes in this chapter proves that sweet desserts without refined sugar, rich-tasting desserts without added fat are not a fantasy. With a bread machine for convenience, you can end a meal with an amazing variety of deeply satisfying, low-fat, sugar-free sweets.

These treats I have developed do not use synthetic sweeteners or fat substitutes. They are made with unsweetened cocoa powder, concentrated juices, and ripe fruits. Fruit that is in season always has the truest flavor. If the fruit is ripe, or even a bit overripe though not spoiled, it will yield optimal sweetness. Cocoa powder, which is basically chocolate minus the cocoa butter, or fat, should be the dark, unsweetened Dutch-process type. It has an intense chocolate taste. Eliminating added sugar and butter allows the flavors of these premium ingredients to come through clearly.

People who must avoid sugar can finish dinner in style with Apple Tart Tatin, Czech Fruit Dumplings, or a lovely Blueberry Tart. The desserts in this chapter deliver a lot of satisfaction to the senses while still fitting into a reduced-calorie diet. The perfume of apples or gingerbread, the bright color of berries, the crispness of biscotti end a meal on a high, clear note with not a tinge of guilt.

Apricot, Ginger, and Wheatberry Bread

This gingery sweet bread needs no topping or filling because it is as tasty as a cookie and as moist as a coffee cake. Serve it with tea or sherry or the classic ginger ale and sherbet punch.

SMALL LOAF (1 POUND)	INGREDIENTS	LARGE LOAF (1½ POUNDS)
1 teaspoon	dry yeast	1½ teaspoons
1¾ cups	bread flour	2⅔ cups
½ cup	whole wheat flour	¾ cup
½ cup	cooked wheatberries (see page 5), coarsely chopped	¾ cup
1 teaspoon	minced fresh ginger	1½ teaspoons
½ teaspoon	salt	¾ teaspoon
2 tablespoons	mashed ripe banana	3 tablespoons
⅔ cup	water	1 cup
¼ cup	chopped dried apricots	⅓ cup

1. Add all ingredients except the dried apricots in the order suggested by your bread machine manual and process on the basic bread cycle according to the manufacturer's directions.

2. Add the dried apricots at the beeper or at the end of the first kneading in machines without a beeper to signal addition of fruit and nuts.

PER (1-OUNCE) SERVING: 83 Calories; .4 gm. Fat; 0 mg. Cholesterol; 4% Calories from Fat

Apple Brown Betty

In winter, just the spicy smell of this bread-based dessert will warm you. We like it for breakfast too with a dollop of yogurt cheese.

Yield: 8 servings   *12 servings*

SMALL LOAF (1 POUND)	INGREDIENTS	LARGE LOAF (1½ POUNDS)
BREAD		
1¼ teaspoons	dry yeast	2 teaspoons
1¾ cups	bread flour	2⅔ cups
½ cup	whole wheat flour	¾ cup
2 teaspoons	ground cinnamon	1 tablespoon
2 teaspoons	ground ginger	1 tablespoon
½ teaspoon	ground cloves	¾ teaspoon
½ teaspoon	salt	¾ teaspoon
¼ cup	mashed ripe banana	⅓ cup
4	dates, minced	6
¾ cup	water	1 cup plus 2 tablespoons
TOPPING		
	Vegetable cooking spray	
6	apples	
¼ cup	apple juice concentrate, thawed	
¼ teaspoon	ground cinnamon	

1. Add all ingredients for the bread in the order suggested by your bread machine manual and process on the basic bread cycle according to the manufacturer's directions.

2. At the end of the baking cycle, remove the bread from the machine and let cool. You'll only need half a small loaf or one-third of a large loaf to make this dessert. Wrap and freeze the remaining bread or eat it. The bread can be made as far ahead as you wish and frozen. Defrost 1 hour before making this dessert. Preheat the oven to 350 degrees.

3. Coat a 9-by-12-inch baking pan with vegetable cooking spray. Cut 4 thin (¼-inch) slices of bread from the loaf. In a blender or food processor, grind the remaining bread into crumbs. Line the bottom of the baking pan with the bread slices. Peel and core the apples and slice into thin wedges. Toss with the apple juice concentrate and cinnamon. Spread over the bread. Sprinkle 1 cup of the bread crumbs over the apples. Bake the crumb-topped apples 45 minutes, or until golden brown on top.

PER (1-OUNCE) SERVING: 138 Calories; .8 gm. Fat; .1 mg. Cholesterol; 5% Calories from Fat

---

Apple Tart Tatin

In Normandy, this tart is made with puff pastry and a great deal of sugar. Sweet bread substitutes for puff pastry here, and the butter is gone. Reducing the sugar lets the apples star.

Yield: 2 (10-inch) tarts, 6 servings each

DOUGH

1½ teaspoons	dry yeast
1¼ cups	bread flour
1 cup	whole wheat flour
½ teaspoon	salt
¼ cup	minced dried figs*
¾ cup	water

TOPPING

	Vegetable cooking spray
1 cup	apple juice concentrate, thawed
6	medium apples

1. Add all ingredients for the dough in the order suggested by your bread machine manual and process on the dough cycle according to the manufacturer's directions.
2. While the dough is being processed, prepare the topping: Coat two 10-inch cake pans, Pyrex pie pans, or ovenproof skillets with vegetable cooking spray. In a small saucepan, boil the apple juice concentrate over high heat until reduced by half,

about 5 minutes. Pour the syrup into the two pans, dividing evenly and swirling if necessary to coat the bottoms. Quarter, core, and peel the apples. Cut each quarter into eighths. Arrange apples in concentric circles in each pan, overlapping the apples.

3. When the dough cycle ends, remove the dough from the machine. Preheat the oven to 350 degrees. Divide the dough in half. On a floured surface with a floured rolling pin, roll each piece into a 10-inch circle. Place each circle on top of a pan of apples.

4. Bake 40 to 45 minutes, or until the tops are brown and bubbling around the edges. Remove from the oven. Let rest 5 minutes, then invert onto a plate larger than the pan so that you will not lose any syrup that drips down the sides. Eat warm, not hot.

*If the figs are hard, pour boiling water over them to soften, then drain well.

PER SERVING: 153 Calories; .9 gm. Fat; 0 mg. Cholesterol; 5% Calories from Fat

Banana Splits

This is playful food and a delicious dessert, sweet but still very low in fat.

Yield: 16 banana splits   *24 banana splits*

SMALL LOAF (1 POUND)	INGREDIENTS	LARGE LOAF (1½ POUNDS)
BREAD		
1 cup	nonfat plain yogurt	1½ cups
1 teaspoon	dry yeast	1½ teaspoons
1¾ cups	bread flour	2⅔ cups
½ cup	whole wheat flour	¾ cup
1 teaspoon	ground cinnamon	1½ teaspoons
½ teaspoon	salt	¾ teaspoon
3 tablespoons	minced dates	¼ cup
½ cup	mashed banana	¾ cup
¼ cup	water	⅓ cup
SAUCE		
½ cup	apple juice concentrate, thawed	¾ cup
2 tablespoons	unsweetened cocoa powder	3 tablespoons
½ teaspoon	vanilla extract	1 teaspoon
4	bananas	6

1. In a cheesecloth-lined strainer or in a coffee filter, drain the yogurt ½ hour.

2. Add all ingredients for the bread in the order suggested by your bread machine manual and process on the basic bread cycle according to the manufacturer's directions.

3. While the bread is baking, make the sauce. Bring the apple juice concentrate to a boil. Stir in the cocoa. Blend well. Remove from the heat and let cool, then add the vanilla.

4. At the end of the baking cycle, remove the bread and let it cool. Slice ½ inch thick. Cut each slice in half. On each dessert plate, place a piece of bread drizzled with chocolate sauce and crowned with banana slices.

PER SERVING: 126 Calories; .6 gm. Fat; .0 mg. Cholesterol; 4% Calories from Fat

Strawberry Shortcake

When berries are at their sweetest and bruise most easily, make this old-fashioned dessert that has been modernized by removing the fat of the traditional biscuit or cake base. A thin, 22-year-old friend loved it, not realizing that it was healthy, too.

Yield: 8 servings *12 servings*

SMALL LOAF (1 POUND)	INGREDIENTS	LARGE LOAF (1½ POUNDS)
DOUGH		
1 teaspoon	dry yeast	1½ teaspoons
1¾ cups	bread flour	2⅔ cups
½ cup	whole wheat flour	¾ cup
2 tablespoons	nonfat dry milk	3 tablespoons
1 tablespoon	apple butter (no sugar added)	1½ tablespoons
¼ cup	mashed ripe banana	⅓ cup
¼ cup	egg substitute	⅓ cup
2 teaspoons	vanilla extract	1 tablespoon
½ teaspoon	salt	¾ teaspoon
⅔ cup	water	1 cup
TOPPING		
2 cups	ripe strawberries	3 cups
2 tablespoons	sugar-free raspberry fruit spread	3 tablespoons

1. Add all ingredients for the dough in the order suggested by your bread machine manual and process on the basic bread cycle according to the manufacturer's directions. The bread can be made up to a day ahead and allowed to cool.

2. Mash the berries in a small nonreactive saucepan. Stir in the fruit spread and bring to a boil. Remove from the heat and let cool, stirring occasionally.

3. Cut bread into 4 (½-inch) slices. Reserve the remaining bread for another use. Trim off the crusts and cut each piece in half. Place a half-slice on each dessert plate. Spoon equal amounts of the berries and their juice over the bread on each plate.

PER SERVING: 90 Calories; .4 gm. Fat; .1 mg. Cholesterol; 4% Calories from Fat

Biscotti with Dried Cherries

SMALL LOAF (1 POUND)	INGREDIENTS	LARGE LOAF (1½ POUNDS)
1¼ teaspoons	dry yeast	2 teaspoons
2 cups	bread flour	3 cups
¼ cup	whole wheat flour	⅓ cup
2 tablespoons	nonfat dry milk	3 tablespoons
1 tablespoon	grated orange zest	1½ tablespoons
1 teaspoon	aniseed	1½ teaspoons
¼ teaspoon	salt	¼ teaspoon
¾ cup plus 2 tablespoons	water	1¼ cups
½ cup	dried cherries or dried cranberries	¾ cup

1. Add all ingredients except the dried cherries or cranberries according to your bread machine manual and process on the basic bread cycle according to the manufacturer's directions.

2. Add the cherries or cranberries at the beeper or at the end of the first kneading in machines without a beeper to signal addition of fruit and nuts. Remove the bread and let cool.

3. Preheat the oven to 350 degrees. Slice the cooled bread, or day-old bread, ½ inch thick. Cut the slices into fingers 1 inch wide. Place on an ungreased baking sheet and toast 20 minutes, or until crisp. The fresher the bread, the longer it needs to toast. Cool and store in airtight containers.

PER (1-OUNCE) SERVING: 82 Calories; .3 gm. Fat; .1 mg. Cholesterol; 4% Calories from Fat

Chocolate Tea Bread

On a scale of one to ten, this is a five in chocolate power; it is mildly bitter and fluffy. For tea, spread apricot or raspberry preserves between thin slices, trim the crusts, and cut into triangles.

SMALL LOAF (1 POUND)	INGREDIENTS	LARGE LOAF (1½ POUNDS)
1½ teaspoons	dry yeast	2 teaspoons
2 cups	bread flour	3 cups
⅓ cup	unsweetened cocoa powder	½ cup
½ teaspoon	salt	¾ teaspoon
¼ cup	minced prunes*	¼ cup plus 2 tablespoons
2	egg whites	3
½ cup	water	¾ cup

Add all ingredients in the order suggested by your bread machine manual and process on the basic bread cycle according to the manufacturer's directions.

*If the prunes are hard, pour boiling water over them to soften, then drain well.

PER (1-OUNCE) SERVING: 75 Calories; .5 gm. Fat; 0 mg. Cholesterol; 6% Calories from Fat

Blueberry Tart

Our preteenage neighbors favored this tart for breakfast. It is an upbeat end to a light summer supper or brunch.

Yield: 2 (10-inch) tarts, 12 servings

DOUGH

8	pitted dates
¾ cup	water
1¼ teaspoons	dry yeast
1½ cups	bread flour
¾ cup	whole wheat flour
½ teaspoon	salt

TOPPING

---

4 cups	fresh blueberries
½ cup	sugar-free blueberry or raspberry fruit spread
1 teaspoon	grated orange zest
¼ teaspoon	ground cinnamon
1½ cups	nonfat plain yogurt
¼ teaspoon	vanilla extract

1. Puree the dates with the water in a food processor or blender until smooth.
2. Add all ingredients for the dough in the order suggested by your bread machine manual and process on the dough cycle according to the manufacturer's directions.
3. While the dough is processing, cook 1 cup of the blueberries with the fruit

spread, orange zest, and cinnamon until the spread dissolves and forms a syrup. Cool and mix with the other 3 cups of berries. Drain the yogurt in a sieve lined with cheesecloth or a coffee filter.

4. At the end of the dough cycle, remove the dough from the machine and divide in half. Preheat the oven to 400 degrees. On a floured board with a floured rolling pin, roll out each piece of dough into a 10-inch circle. Set each piece on a large baking sheet, loosely cover, and let rest in a draft-free place 10 minutes. Bake for 10 minutes, turn the dough rounds over, and bake another 10 minutes. Remove from the oven and let cool.

5. Mix the drained yogurt with the vanilla and spread ½ of the mixture on each crust. Top each with half of the blueberry mixture. Cut into wedges to serve.

PER SERVING: 151 Calories; .6 gm. Fat; 0 mg. Cholesterol; 4% Calories from Fat

Devilish Chocolate Bread

I love this bread. If you like chocolate, indulge in this low-fat version, even serve a slice with low-fat vanilla ice cream. It has a deeply chocolate flavor, grown up and devilishly delicious.

SMALL LOAF (1 POUND)	INGREDIENTS	LARGE LOAF (1½ POUNDS)
¾ cup	apple juice concentrate, thawed	1 cup
½ cup	unsweetened cocoa powder	¾ cup
1¼ teaspoons	dry yeast	2 teaspoons
1¾ cups	bread flour	2⅔ cups
½ cup	whole wheat flour	¾ cup
2 teaspoons	grated orange zest	1 tablespoon
½ teaspoon	salt	¾ teaspoon
1 teaspoon	vanilla extract	1½ teaspoons
¼ cup	water	⅓ cup

1. In a small saucepan, bring ½ (⅔) cup of the apple juice concentrate to a boil over medium heat. Blend in the cocoa, stirring until smooth. Remove from the heat and let cool to room temperature.

2. Add all the ingredients including the cocoa syrup and remaining apple juice concentrate in the order suggested by your bread machine manual and process on the basic bread cycle according to the manufacturer's directions.

PER (1-OUNCE) SERVING: 97 Calories; .7 gm. Fat; 0 mg. Cholesterol; 6% Calories from Fat

Russian Coffee Cake

This is as rich as it gets without butter and egg yolks. These fruit-filled squares, fresh and spicy, will make a brunch or tea a banquet.

SMALL LOAF (1 POUND)	INGREDIENTS	LARGE LOAF (1½ POUNDS)
1 recipe for challah dough (page 54), prepared through Step 2		
½ teaspoon	ground cinnamon	¾ teaspoon
½ teaspoon	ground ginger	¾ teaspoon
½ cup	raisins	¾ cup
½ cup	dried cherries or currants	¾ cup
1	egg white, beaten	1

1. When the dough cycle ends, remove the dough from the machine. On a floured surface with a floured rolling pin, roll the dough into a 9-by-12-inch rectangle. Sprinkle the spices over the dough. Cut the dough into thirds. Sprinkle the raisins over one piece of dough. Top with another piece of dough. Sprinkle the dried cherries or currants over the second layer of dough. Place the third piece on top, spiced side-down. Pinch the edges together to seal in the fruits.

2. Roll out the filled dough into a 9-by-12-inch rectangle, being careful not to lose the fruits. Place the dough on a nonstick baking sheet. Brush the top with the egg white. Score the top into squares to make the cake easier to cut when baked. Cover and let rise in a draft-free place 30 minutes, until doubled in size.

3. While the dough is rising, preheat the oven to 350 degrees. Bake 20 to 25 minutes, or until golden brown.

PER (1-OUNCE) SERVING: 99 Calories; .3 gm. Fat; 0 mg. Cholesterol; 3% Calories from Fat

Fruit-Filled Danish Pastries

The smell and taste of these seemingly rich pastries will warm the coldest winter afternoon or dreariest morning, or provide a lovely touch of sweetness with your evening coffee.

Yield: 9 pastries   *12 pastries*

DOUGH

2	saffron threads	3
1 cup	water	1½ cups
1½ teaspoons	dry yeast	2¼ teaspoons
2 cups	bread flour	3 cups
2 tablespoons	minced prunes*	3 tablespoons
2 tablespoons	grated lemon zest	3 tablespoons
1 teaspoon	ground cardamom	1½ teaspoons
½ teaspoon	salt	¾ teaspoon
2	egg whites	3

FILLING

1 cup	water	1½ cups
½ cup	dried apricots	¾ cup
½ cup	sugar-free apricot fruit spread	¾ cup

1. Bring the water to a boil, add the saffron, and let cool.

2. Add all ingredients for the dough in the order suggested by your bread machine manual and process on the dough cycle according to the manufacturer's directions.

3. For the filling, bring the 1 (1½) cup(s) of water to a boil, add the dried apricots, and remove from the heat. Let the apricots cool to room temperature in the water, then drain well. If the apricots are whole, separate them into halves.

4. At the end of the dough cycle, remove the dough from the machine. (The dough can be refrigerated overnight or for a few hours at this point.) On a floured board with a floured rolling pin, roll the dough into a 12-inch square or a 12-by-16-inch rectangle for the larger amount. Cut into 9 (12) squares. Place equal portions of apricots and fruit spread in the center of each square. Pull up the points of 2 opposite corners over the fruit and press together. Pinch the other pair of corners to make a square package enclosing the filling. Place the Danish pastries 2 inches apart on a nonstick baking sheet (s). Cover loosely and let rise in a draft-free place about 25 minutes.

5. While the pastries are rising, preheat the oven to 375 degrees. When they have doubled in size, bake until golden brown, about 15 to 20 minutes.

*If the prunes are hard, pour boiling water over them to soften, then drain well.

PER (1-OUNCE) SERVING: 179 Calories; .6 gm. Fat; 0 mg. Cholesterol; 3% Calories from Fat

Czech Fruit Dumplings

After a concert or ice skating or roller blading on a crisp day, these dumplings will warm you. They are comforting as the center of a weekend brunch or as dessert after dinner.

Yield: 12 dumplings, 12 servings

DOUGH

1½ teaspoons	dry yeast
2 cups	bread flour
2 tablespoons	wheat bran
2 tablespoons	nonfat dry milk
½ teaspoon	salt
½ cup	mashed potato
½ cup	water

FILLING AND TOPPING

6	very ripe prune plums
	or
1½	ripe sweet pears, such as Bartlett
¼ teaspoon	ground cinnamon

1. Add all ingredients for the dough in the order suggested by your bread machine manual and process on the dough cycle according to the manufacturer's directions.
2. Meanwhile, cut the plums in half and remove the pits; or quarter the pears lengthwise and cut out the cores, then cut each quarter crosswise into 2 chunks.

---

3. At the end of the dough cycle, remove the dough from the machine. Divide into 12 equal pieces. Place a plum half or a piece of pear in the center of each piece of dough. Pull up the edges of the dough around the fruit and pinch together tightly to form fruit-filled balls. Place the balls 3 inches apart on a nonstick baking sheet and press down to flatten. Cover loosely and let rise in a draft-free place about 20 minutes, until doubled.

4. Preheat the oven to 350 degrees. Bake 20 minutes, or until the dumplings are golden brown. Sprinkle the cinnamon over the dumplings. Eat warm or at room temperature.

PER SERVING: 109 Calories; .6 gm. Fat; .1 mg. Cholesterol; 5% Calories from Fat

Fruity Tea Bread

The natural sweetness of fruit makes this bread very satisfying for afternoon or late-night snacking. Cool completely and slice thin.

SMALL LOAF (1 POUND)	INGREDIENTS	LARGE LOAF (1½ POUNDS)
1 teaspoon	dry yeast	1½ teaspoons
1¾ cups	bread flour	2⅔ cups
⅓ cup	whole wheat flour	½ cup
2 tablespoons	nonfat dry milk	3 tablespoons
½ teaspoon	salt	¾ teaspoon
1	egg white(s)	2
¾ cup	water	1 cup
½ cup	dried cherries	⅔ cup
½ cup	raisins	⅔ cup

1. Add all ingredients except the cherries and raisins according to your bread machine manual and process on the basic bread cycle according to the manufacturer's directions.

2. Add the dried cherries and raisins at the beeper or at the end of the first kneading in machines without a beeper to signal addition of fruit and nuts.

NOTE: In some machines the fruit will congregate around the sides of the bread, making a caramelized sweet crust.

PER (1-OUNCE) SERVING: 95 Calories; .4 gm. Fat; .1 mg. Cholesterol; 4% Calories from Fat

Gingerbread

On cold days with hot chocolate or tea, this bread makes a fine snack. It is also a lunch-box favorite. If you can afford a little sweetener, the molasses here contributes a traditional gingerbread taste. If not, the apple butter yields a milder sweet and spicy bread.

SMALL LOAF (1 POUND)	INGREDIENTS	LARGE LOAF (1½ POUNDS)
1¼ teaspoons	dry yeast	2 teaspoons
1½ cups	bread flour	2¼ cups
¾ cup	whole wheat flour	1 cup plus 2 tablespoons
2 tablespoons	molasses or apple butter (no sugar added)	3 tablespoons
¼ cup	minced prunes*	⅓ cup
1½ teaspoons	ground cinnamon	2¼ teaspoons
1½ teaspoons	ground ginger	2¼ teaspoons
½ teaspoon	salt	¾ teaspoon
¼ cup	egg substitute	⅓ cup
½ cup	water	¾ cup

Add all ingredients in the order suggested by your bread machine manual and process on the basic bread cycle according to the manufacturer's directions.

*If the prunes are hard, pour boiling water over them to soften, then drain well.

PER (1-OUNCE) SERVING: 82 Calories; .3 gm. Fat; 0 mg. Cholesterol; 4% Calories from Fat

Pineapple and Jalapeño Bread

SMALL LOAF (1 POUND)	INGREDIENTS	LARGE LOAF (1½ POUNDS)
1 teaspoon	dry yeast	1½ teaspoons
1¾ cups	bread flour	2⅔ cups
½ cup	whole wheat flour	¾ cup
¼ cup	mashed potato	⅓ cup
1 teaspoon	grated orange zest	1½ teaspoons
1 tablespoon	minced fresh jalapeño pepper or ½ (¾) teaspoon crushed hot pepper	1½ tablespoons
½ teaspoon	salt	¾ teaspoon
⅔ cup	water	¾ cup
½ cup	fresh or drained canned unsweetened pineapple chunks	¾ cup

1. Add all ingredients except pineapple in the order suggested by your bread machine manual and process on the basic bread cycle according to the manufacturer's directions.

2. Add the pineapple at the beeper or at the end of the first kneading in machines without a beeper to signal addition of fruits and nuts.

PER (1-OUNCE) SERVING: 75 Calories; .3 gm. Fat; 0 mg. Cholesterol; 4% Calories from Fat

Orange and Prune Bread

Prunes proclaim their undervalued tart, fruity flavor as well as contribute the softening property in this bread. Perfumed with orange, it tastes good enough for tea, breakfast, or even dessert.

SMALL LOAF (1 POUND)	INGREDIENTS	LARGE LOAF (1½ POUNDS)
1½ teaspoons	dry yeast	2¼ teaspoons
1¾ cups	bread flour	2⅔ cups
½ cup	whole wheat flour	¾ cup
1 tablespoon	grated orange zest	1½ tablespoons
½ teaspoon	salt	¾ teaspoon
½ cup	minced prunes*	¾ cup
¾ cup plus 2 tablespoons	water	1¼ cups

Add all ingredients in the order suggested by your bread machine manual and process on the basic bread cycle according to the manufacturer's directions.

*If the prunes are hard, pour boiling water over them to soften, then drain well.

PER (1-OUNCE) SERVING: 80 Calories; .3 gm. Fat; 0 mg. Cholesterol; 4% Calories from Fat

Spice Cake

This rich tea cake manages to be so low in fat because it is jam-packed with fruits and spices.

SMALL LOAF (1 POUND)	INGREDIENTS	LARGE LOAF (1½ POUNDS)
¼ cup	pitted dates	⅓ cup
¾ cup	water	1 cup plus 2 tablespoons
1 teaspoon	dry yeast	1½ teaspoons
1½ cups	bread flour	2¼ cups
¾ cup	whole wheat flour	1 cup plus 2 tablespoons
2 teaspoons	ground cinnamon	1 tablespoon
1 teaspoon	ground ginger	1½ teaspoons
1 teaspoon	ground cardamom	1½ teaspoons
½ teaspoon	ground cloves	¾ teaspoon
½ teaspoon	ground allspice	¾ teaspoon
½ teaspoon	salt	¾ teaspoon
2 tablespoons	pumpkin puree	3 tablespoons

1. In a food processor, puree the dates with the water until smooth.
2. Add all ingredients including the date puree in the order suggested by your bread machine manual and process on the basic bread cycle according to the manufacturer's directions.

PER (1-OUNCE) SERVING: 76 Calories; .3 gm. Fat; 0 mg. Cholesterol; 4% Calories from Fat

Chapter Six

Bread Again: Using Leftover Loaves

Not everyone uses a whole loaf of bread each day. When you have leftovers, save them to create an entirely new recipe. Making a soup, hors d'oeuvre, or dessert out of what might have been a throwaway is like finding a wad of dollars in the pocket of a jacket. It will not make you rich, but it can give you a great deal of pleasure.

The Portuguese make soup from leftover bread. Italians make it into a salad called *panzanella* and an hors d'oeuvre called *bruschetta*. In France, stale bread is transformed into a charlotte, a kind of bread pudding. Here are low-fat, sugar-free versions of these recipes and more.

If you are freezing the leftover bread, slice it first, then wrap it tightly in plastic wrap and put the wrapped bread in a plastic bag. If you are toasting the bread for the second use, do not bother to defrost it before toasting. The center will stay softer while the outside becomes crisp.

These recipes for using bread again—and again—are still low in fat and sugar-free, good for your health and your budget, and excellent for the environment.

Bread Pudding

This light, winter dessert is best served warm with apricot or raspberry puree on the side. Use day-old bread.

Yield: *12 servings*   *18 servings*

	Vegetable cooking spray	
1 (1-pound) loaf	Pineapple and Sweet Potato Bread (page 36)	1 (1½-pound) loaf
1 quart	skim milk	1½ quarts
2 teaspoons	vanilla extract	1 tablespoon
1 teaspoon	ground nutmeg	1½ teaspoons
½ teaspoon	ground cinnamon	¾ teaspoon
4	pitted dates, minced	6
1 cup	currants or raisins	1½ cups
2 teaspoons	grated orange zest	1 tablespoon
4	egg whites	6

1. Preheat the oven to 350 degrees. Spray a 9-by-12-inch pan with vegetable cooking spray. Tear the bread into 1-inch pieces.

2. In a large bowl, combine the milk, vanilla, nutmeg, cinnamon, dates, currants, and orange zest. Pour the mixture over the bread and let stand ½ hour.

3. Beat the egg whites until stiff. Fold into the bread mixture, being careful not to overmix and deflate the egg whites. Spoon the mixture into the baking pan and bake 1 hour, or until the top is brown.

PER SERVING: 193 Calories; .8 gm. Fat; 2 mg. Cholesterol; 4% Calories from Fat

Bread Salad

Save day-old bread or make some one day ahead especially for this Italian salad, called panzanella.

Yield: 10 servings   *15 servings*

1 (1-pound) loaf	Country Bread (page 58) or Simple Sourdough Bread (page 75)	1 (1½-pound) loaf
3 pounds	very ripe tomatoes	5 pounds
½ pound	red onions, very thinly sliced	¾ pound
½ cup	red wine vinegar	¾ cup
¼ teaspoon	salt	½ teaspoon
¼ teaspoon	freshly ground black pepper	¼ teaspoon
¼ cup	chopped parsley	⅓ cup
¼ cup	basil leaves	⅓ cup

1. Tear the bread into 1-inch pieces. Place in a bowl with cold water 5 minutes. Drain and squeeze out as much moisture as possible. Place the bread in a large salad bowl.

2. Chop the tomatoes into ½-inch dice. Add to the bread. Separate the onion slices into rings and scatter over the tomatoes. Add the vinegar, salt, and pepper. Toss to mix well. Divide among at least 10 (15) salad plates and sprinkle the parsley on top. Snip large basil leaves and sprinkle on top. Use small leaves for garnish.

PER SERVING: 108 Calories; .7 gm. Fat; 0 mg. Cholesterol; 5% Calories from Fat

Bread Soup

On a cold winter night, a few crusts of bread and some staples from the cupboard turn into nourishing comfort food. Every Mediterranean country has its version of Bread Soup from the Portuguese Caldo Gallego *to the French* Le Soupe aux Choux.

Yield: 8 servings

1	Whole Wheat Baguette (page 88)
3 cups	beef bouillon
3 cups	water
1	medium leek (white and tender green), cleaned and chopped
1	medium onion, chopped
2 cups	chopped cabbage
2	medium carrots, chopped
1 cup	canned plum tomatoes, drained and chopped
1	garlic clove, minced
	Coarsely ground black pepper
	Chopped parsley or grated Parmesan cheese, as accompaniment

1. Preheat the oven to 350 degrees. Cut the bread into 1½-inch cubes and place on a baking sheet. Toast in the oven 10 to 15 minutes, or until golden.
2. Bring the bouillon and water to a boil. And the leek, onion, cabbage, carrots, tomatoes, garlic, and pepper to taste. Cover and simmer for at least an hour.

3. Place the bread cubes in a soup tureen. Add the vegetables and broth. Cover and wrap in a thick Turkish towel. Let stand at least 5 minutes before serving. Sprinkle each serving with chopped parsley or grated Parmesan cheese.

PER SERVING: 110 Calories; 1 gm. Fat; 0 mg. Cholesterol; 8% Calories from Fat

Bruschetta of Summer Tomato and Basil

The essence of Italian food is its honesty. Could an hors d'oeuvre be more forthright than this bruschetta of toasted bread, ripe tomatoes, and fresh herbs?

Yield: 24 servings

6 slices	Italian Sourdough Bread (page 72) or *Pane Rustico* (page 65)
1	garlic clove, cut in half
1½ cups	diced ripe tomatoes
6	basil leaves

1. Slice the bread ½ inch thick. Cut each slice into 4 pieces. Toast briefly on both sides under the broiler or in a toaster oven. Rub each piece of toasted bread with the cut side of the garlic.

2. Top each bruschetta with 1 tablespoon of diced tomatoes. With a scissors, snip the basil so that a few pieces fall on each bruschetta for garnish.

PER SERVING: 28 Calories; .3 gm. Fat; 0 mg. Cholesterol; 11% Calories from Fat

Crostini with White Beans

In Tuscany, the ubiquitous crostini, *toasted slabs of bread, are slathered with liver paste. White beans with sun-dried tomato brings this hors d'oeuvre into the 90s.*

Yield: 24 servings

6 (½-inch-thick) slices	*Pane Rustico* (page 65)
1 cup	canned white beans, rinsed and drained
¼ cup	chopped sun-dried tomatoes*
½	garlic clove, minced
1 teaspoon	fresh or dried rosemary
⅛ teaspoon	freshly ground black pepper

1. Preheat the oven to 350 degrees. Cut each slice of bread into 4 pieces. Bake 15 minutes to make crostini.

2. Mash the beans. Mix in the sun-dried tomatoes, garlic, rosemary, and pepper.

3. Spoon the bean mixture on top of the toasted crostini, dividing evenly, or serve the toasts and topping separately and let guests make their own hors d'oeuvre.

*Pour boiling water over the sun-dried tomato halves. Soak 10 minutes, drain, and let cool to room temperature. With a scissors, snip into ¼-inch pieces. Do not use tomatoes that are reconstituted and packed in oil for this recipe.

PER SERVING: 35 Calories; .2 gm. Fat; 0 mg. Cholesterol; 5% Calories from Fat

Frega

Frega *are toasts rubbed pink with a cut tomato. More portable and even simpler than* bruschetta, *these morsels travel well to picnics and add to an antipasto platter. Or serve with grilled fish or barbecued vegetables.*

Yield: 24 servings

6 (½-inch-thick) slices	Country Bread (page 58) or *Pane Rustico* (page 65)
1	garlic clove
1	very ripe tomato
	Salt and freshly ground black pepper

1. Toast the bread briefly on each side under a broiler or in a toaster oven.
2. Cut the garlic clove in half. Slice the tomato in half. Rub one side of the toast with the cut side of the garlic. Rub it with the tomato until the bread becomes pink. Sprinkle with salt and freshly ground pepper to taste.

PER SERVING: 26 Calories; .2 gm. Fat; 0 mg. Cholesterol; 5% Calories from Fat

Pineapple Upside-Down Toasts

End a brunch or dinner with this satisfyingly sweet and gooey dessert.

Yield: 8 servings

	Vegetable cooking spray
½ cup	apple juice concentrate, thawed
8 slices	pineapple*
8 slices	sweet bread (Banana Chutney Bread, page 95, or Pumpkin and Sweet Apple Bread, page 138)

1. Preheat the oven to 400 degrees. Lightly coat 8 muffin cups with vegetable cooking spray. In a small saucepan, boil apple juice concentrate over heat until reduced by half. Cover the bottom of each muffin cup with ½ tablespoon reduced concentrate. Place 1 round of pineapple in each cup.

2. Slice the bread about ½ inch thick. Cut a round the size of a muffin cup from each slice and place the rounds on top of the pineapple.

3. Bake 25 minutes. Put a plate on top of the muffin cup or tin and invert to unmold. Let cool before serving.

*Pineapple should be fresh or canned in juice, not in heavy syrup. If pineapple is canned, drain it well.

PER SERVING: 175 Calories; 1 gm. Fat; .1 mg. Cholesterol; 6% Calories from Fat

Bibliography

American Heart Association Cookbook. New York: American Heart Association, 1993.

Bread Bakers Guild of America Newsletter. Pittsburgh, 1994.

Bumgartner, Marlene Anne. *The Book of Whole Grains*. New York: St. Martin's Press, 1976.

Carper, Jean. *The Food Pharmacy Guide to Good Eating*. New York: Bantam, 1991.

Corriher, Shirley O. "Fat Expertise for the Cook." Louisville, Kentucky: International Association of Cooking Professionals, 1993.

Great Tastes, Healthy Cooking from Canyon Ranch. Tucson, Arizona: Canyon Ranch, 1992.

Harvard Women's Health Watch. Boston: Harvard Medical School Health Publications Program, 1994.

Madison, Deborah. *The Savory Way*. New York: Bantam, 1990.

Madison, Deborah and Brown, Edward Espe. *Greens*. New York: Bantam, 1987.

Netzer, Corinne T. *The Complete Book of Food Counts*. New York: Dell, 1994.

Ornish, Dean. *Eat More, Weigh Less*. New York: HarperCollins, 1987.

Pennington, Jean A. T. *Food Values of Portions Commonly Used.* 15th edition. New York: HarperCollins, 1989.

Purdy, Susan G. *Have Your Cake and Eat It, Too.* New York: Morrow, 1993.

Scicolone, Michele. *The Antipasto Table.* New York: Morrow, 1991.

Tufts Nutrition Newsletter. New York: Tufts University Diet and Nutrition Newsletter, 1993–1994.

Index